MEDICARE

NIGHTMARE
The Great Australian Tragedy

By Dal Ouba

In the loving memory of my Angels and

other victims of the Medicare Nightmare

The people and situations described in this book are real, but the names and other identifying details have been altered. Any similarity between an individual, business or situation described in this book and any real person, place or event is purely coincidental.

ACCELERATE AUSTRALIA

First published in Australia in 2016

By Accelerate Australia, Sydney

ABN 61 640 942 931

www.AccelerateAustralia.net.au

Written, edited and illustrated by Dalal Oubani

Medicare Nightmare: The Great Australian Tragedy

ISBN 978-0-9953689-0-3

Preface

The lack of access to the right medical information and as a result adequate medical care at the right time means that there is a silent portion of the Australian population suffering from the dilemma known as 'the Medicare Nightmare.'

Yet, this nightmare is not just a personal nightmare but a national one as well as poor information flow in our healthcare system and society as a whole results in increasing medical errors, escalating medical costs associated with improper medical care and an overburdened healthcare system, impacting on our national wealth and health.

Incorporating case-study analysis, this book tackles how this poor information flow occurs allowing all key stakeholders in the healthcare system to take more responsibility for not just their personal health and wealth but that of their nation too. It is only through creating more community awareness in our society on the great Medicare Nightmare that we can increase our chances of alleviating the personal suffering and costs incurred by those unfortunate victims trapped in the Medicare Nightmare and reveal the hidden impact and costs these collective nightmares have on our society as a whole.

Whether one is working in the medical field, health insurance, government or medical legal field, the Medicare Nightmare is a great eye opener on how this lack of efficient information flow or awareness dooms our healthcare system to failure and undermines the foundation of our nation's wealth - its health. Students in secondary and tertiary education must also be aware of how their education has failed to prepare them to make the most important decisions for their future when trying to effectively manage their health.

The information contained in this book is strictly the authors' personal opinion and every effort has been made to present factual, accurate information as seen through the authors' personal experiences and education. The information contained in this book should be used as a reference and as a reader you may agree or disagree with the information and ideas in this book. You should discuss all health care issues with your private physician and your healthcare professional should monitor your personal healthcare. Neither the author nor the publishers shall be liable or responsible for any loss or damage allegedly arising from any information or suggestion in this book. This is because every individual's health is unique and they must make the ultimate decision regarding their health treatment plans.

I would like to thank those who have supported the production of this book and have given permission for copyrighted information to be reused in order to improve the efficiency of our healthcare system and ensure that more Australians are saved from being trapped in the great Medicare Nightmare.

The Medicare Nightmare

Chapter One: Understanding the Medicare Nightmare

The existence and sustainability of our health system
depends heavily on the efficiency of the Medicare scheme-
the commonwealth funded health insurance scheme
that provides free or subsidized healthcare services to
the Australian population. Medicare also provides free
hospital services for public patients in public hospitals,
subsidizes private patients for hospital services and
provides benefits for out of hospital medical services such
as consultations with GP's or specialists. Operated by the
government authority, Medicare Australia, Medicare was
introduced February 1984 and is the major component of
the commonwealth health budget (43%). In 2007-2008,
it cost the Australian economy $18.3 billion to run, with
many professional bodies and businesses questioning the
sustainability of supporting Medicare due to its increasing
impact on national GDP. Until now, discourse on the
inefficiency of our health system has been reduced to
discussions on ambiguous figures and statistics, focusing
attention on the symptoms of our ailing health system
while leading to a poor understanding of the catastrophic
consequences our inefficient health system has on
individuals, other government systems and the nation
as a whole. This leads to a *Medicare Nightmare,* an
individual and national tragedy that can in many ways be
preventable through creating greater public awareness and
focus on the real tragedy behind what has been passed off
as mere funding issues, due to public discussions on our

healthcare system becoming essentially politicized and non-productive.

The *Medicare Nightmare* is a reality that many Australians face, yet they are unable to describe the causation behind their misery and instead face deep self-regret. Some put it down to bad luck, others to random events that have happened in their lives, failing to draw a link between the contributory factors in their lives that have led to their devastating personal costs and economic hardship. They fail to see how poor information flow on medical treatments in their society have contributed to their misery. To some people their experience of the Medicare Nightmare is literally an abyss on earth.

To illustrate how pervading the effects of the Medicare Nightmare actually are, a case-study based on a real victim will be used to explore exactly what it is that disempowers us to make good medical decisions in our life and demonstrate how some of us can accidently find ourselves magnets to medical mismanagement leading to being caught up in the depth of the Medicare Nightmare. However, you will rarely find such stories acknowledged in any health statistics books or medical books. Similar to the thousands of Australians caught up in the Medicare Nightmare, there are many gaps within the accountability of our health system that render such stories and experiences as invisible and unknown to mainstream society.

So, what is the 'Medicare Nightmare' you might ask? The Medicare Nightmare (MN) is concerned with a patient's lack of access to crucial, pivotal health information and as a result adequate medical treatment in a timely manner due to predominantly external factors in society that jeopardize a patient's ability to make sound, informed decisions in the health system. This poor access to empowering information results in disastrous choices and repercussions for both the individual and society as a whole. The MN can be defined as a physical, financial, emotional, spiritual and psychological crisis triggered as a result of one or more improper and inadequate medical treatments that to lead to an ongoing cascade of health woes, inflicting significant personal and national loss. It is a personal as well as a national nightmare. It is a physical nightmare as the human body is forced to endure numerous rounds or even endless rounds of surgery, creating greater physical risks and more experiences of harm that are detrimental in the long run to the individuals health. This physical nightmare is concerned not just with the inevitable outcome of more surgeries but the resulting need for more risky diagnostic procedures and medicines with significant side-effects, pounding the fragile human body and reducing its dignity to that of a guinea pig in a lab. It is a financial nightmare as the victim not only becomes less able to earn a living and maintain their living standards but is also faced with skyrocketing medical costs, often higher than what they can afford. They often struggle with balancing work commitments with their health and finding the means to pay specialised doctors to help them escape their traumatic dilemma. It is an emotional nightmare as the victim often finds themselves alienated with the support of their friends waning over time due to their deteriorating health affecting their ability to sustain social relationships. It is a spiritual nightmare as repeated tragic events whose occurrence is often reduced to luck, compromise an individual's faith and hope for healing, stirring every atheist bone in an individual's body. Finally, it is a psychological nightmare as the victims mental strength is tested to the extreme, increasing their risks of having mental illnesses such as depression and post-traumatic disorder.

For a few, it ends with death- a pitiful death with no apologies from the system that inflicted it in the first place. The inefficiency behind the Medicare Nightmare is not just due to medical negligence or the patient being under the care of the wrong health professional. Inefficiency within our healthcare system is merely symptomatic and forces one to consider why patients find themselves-too often trapped in risky health dilemmas. At the centre of the Medicare Nightmare is the poor information flow within the healthcare system in our society which causes individuals to significantly err when making the most important decisions of their lives, that impact on their quality of life and wellbeing.

For some individuals, the nightmare eventually subsides but for others it continues for years or even decades. For most, it either results in a temporary or even permanent loss of quality of life as they not only waste the most precious years of their life seeking medical treatment but they also risk losing everything in life that they cherish- their close relationships, marriage, career and family.

The simplest way to understand the variety of experiences endured is to perceive the Medicare Nightmare as lying on a continuum with the least severe scenarios on the left. This continuum reveals that even though most individuals find themselves towards the left side of the continuum with a minimal impact on the quality of their lives, the *collective cost* of having so *many* patients continuing to visit medical practitioners and specialists to solve the *same* medical problem that *should* have been resolved within the first few visits easily becomes costly over a given period of time. The continuum suggests a fluid state, rather than a permanent status as where one lies on the continuum can change due to either the patient having their health issue resolved- or exacerbated during the process of seeking adequate medical treatment.

The following are only examples of the continuum and reveal the incredibly diverse experiences or Medicare Nightmares and extent of the losses (financial and personal). They are not exclusive examples but simply reveal that everyone's experience of the Medicare Nightmare is unique with most patients being unaware that they have indeed become victims of a system plagued with inefficient information flow between end-users and providers.

The continuum can best be visualized as below:

<u>The Medicare Nightmare Continuum</u>

<u>Stage One:</u> Significantly, 30% seek medical treatment over a short period of time (mnths – yrs) to solve moderately significant health problems. They suffer from mild to moderate stress but appear relatively healthy.

<u>Stage Three</u>: Around 20% seek medical treatment over a short period of time (mnths –yrs) to solve serious health problems that are decreasing the quality of their lives. They suffer from severe stress and moderate depression, due to all aspects of the nightmare being strongly manifested. Their suffering is relatively observable.

<u>Stage Five</u>: Approximately, 10% continue to seek medical treatment over a variable period of time to solve a chronic health problem that has destroyed their quality of life. All aspects of the nightmare are strongly manifested and their suffering is very observable. The irreversible morbidity of this group leads to a high mortality rate.

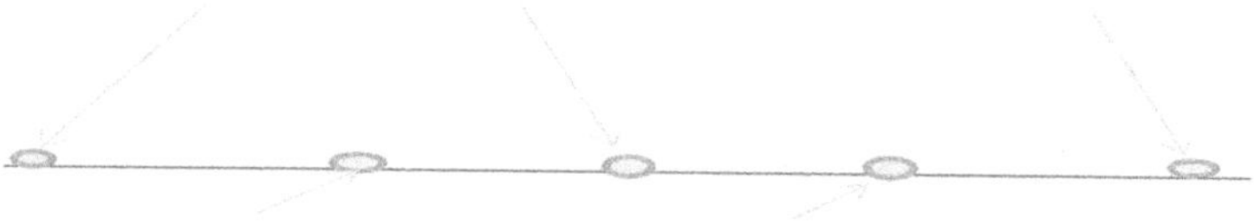

<u>Stage Two</u>: An estimated 25% continue to seek medical treatment over a short period of time (mnths –yrs) to solve a moderately severe health problem that affects their quality of life. They suffer from moderate to severe stress, due to all aspects of the nightmare being manifested. Their suffering is relatively observable.

<u>Stage Four</u>: Nearly, 15% continue to seek medical treatment over a prolonged period of time (yrs) to solve a serious health problem that has decreased their quality of life. They suffer from severe stress and depression, due to all aspects of the nightmare being strongly manifested. Their suffering is quite observable.

As we move from the left side to the right side of the continuum, all aspects of suffering (emotional, psychological, physical, spiritual and financial) increase with the overall quality of life decreasing as a result.

Although one can easily dedicate an entire book to examples and stories of Medicare Nightmares, I will only use examples to demonstrate each part of the continuum, using examples of real individuals I have met that have endured some version of the Medicare Nightmare; some suffering from more catastrophic and severe consequences than others. It is significant to note that none of these people have sued or been mentioned in any statistical health mismanagement report for various reasons. For confidentiality purposes, I have changed their names below.

Stage One of the Medicare Nightmare:

Tina's seven year old son Sam suffers from moderate to severe ongoing chest pain which affects his health and generally accompanies a high fever. Tina has sought the advice of different specialists since he was three, who have all given her a different diagnosis, ranging from pneumonia to Mediterranean fever and even suggested imperfections in her child's spine. Sam suffers from periodic episodes of pain every two months, meaning he takes extra time off school and cannot sometimes participate in normal children's activities such as play or sports. Her son usually cries from the pain, however most specialists she has seen simply recommend trialling different types of antibiotics. Sam otherwise is a friendly happy child who lives a normal life although shy when making friends. This moderately severe health problem- when it strikes, decreases the quality of life for both the parent and the child who continually have to encounter endless expensive rounds of seeking medical advice to find an appropriate cure. Both the parent and the child suffer from mild to moderate stress as a consequence but appear to the outside observer relatively healthy.

<u>Stage Two of the Medicare Nightmare:</u>

Joe is a 45 year old labourer who suffers from a knee problem and was convinced by a specialist that he should not just operate on the problematic knee but his good knee too as a precaution in order to prevent future problems. Not only did the knee surgery fail to cure Joe's problematic knee but it also created new pain in his good knee. As a result, Joe had to then seek medical treatment for both knees visiting different types of medical professionals for both pain management and physiotherapy. This moderately severe health problem decreased the quality of Joe's life as he suffered from moderate to severe stress at times, due to the Medicare Nightmare affecting aspects of his life such as career and family. His suffering is relatively observable to the outside observer as Joe sometimes limps due to his pain, takes sick leave often and avoids many social activities.

<u>Stage Three of the Medicare Nightmare:</u>

Mark noticed that he had a swollen thigh and saw various doctors over a period of 7 months who all insisted that his swollen thigh and pain was due to a mere infection. Mark was given antibiotics but the swelling and pain continued to worsen. He was finally sent to perform a CT scan which revealed that he had a rare Myxoid Liposarcoma which had grown to the size of a soccer ball. Marks surgery to remove the cancerous tissue was successful; however, due to the incredible size the sarcoma had grown, a significant amount of muscle tissue also had to be taken out leading to a weakness in Marks right leg. This late cancer diagnosis decreased the quality of Marks life as he could no longer apply for most jobs he was qualified for, which required constantly standing up or walking around. Mark as a result of his reduced employment prospects, suffers from severe stress and moderate depression due to all aspects of the Medicare Nightmare being strongly manifested in his life. His suffering is relatively observable to the outside observer.

Another example of stage three of the Medicare Nightmare is Pam. Pam, who is underweight and born with a weak cervix, suffers from cervical incompetence. Pam was encouraged after losing twins that a trans-vaginal cerclage would be adequate enough to save future pregnancies. The obstetrician who insisted on this type of cerclage had only a success rate of 60% in this area although he held a high position in obstetrics and was considered an expert with infertility management. As a result, Pam continued to suffer for several more years, burying babies and having to overcome her continuous traumatic losses after a second surgeon also convinced her to retry the same disastrous type of cerclage. This decreased the quality of Pam's life as she spent 3 years of her life bedridden and mourning due to the poor cerclage placements she was given. Pam suffered from severe stress and moderate depression due to all aspects of the Medicare Nightmare being strongly manifested in her life. Her suffering is relatively observable to the outside observer as visible signs of stress and depression are embedded in Pams face. Pam though finally did find the right surgeon to perform the right type of cervical stitch (a Shirodkar) suitable for her needs and was able to finally have her two children.

<u>Stage Four of the Medicare Nightmare:</u>

Alison's story is similar to Pams as she also needed a cerclage to prevent second trimester miscarriages. The difference is that Alison was not born with a weak cervix but had her cervix significantly damaged by doctors during a routine D & C (dilation and curettage) procedure following an incomplete miscarriage. Alison was prone to suffering from miscarriages due to being inflicted with severe Asherman's Syndrome during a disastrous C-section with her first child which destroyed both the endometrial lining of her womb and cervix. The damage was so significant that even with a good cerclage, Alison still had high chances of premature labour and having children born with disabilities as a result. Alison's career was destroyed as she was constantly bedridden even with the cerclage in place leading to significant emotional and financial stress for her family. All future pregnancies were to be classified as high risk, with Alison suffering from more than five traumatising, consecutive miscarriages. Alison's marriage was also constantly at risk due to the considerable amount of stress it inflicted on both her and her partner. Alison sought medical advice over a decade - a prolonged period of time with the quality of her life significantly affected. She suffered from severe stress, post-traumatic stress disorder and severe depression due to all aspects of the Medicare Nightmare being strongly manifested in her life. Her suffering was very obvious to the outside observer. **Due to the pervading effects of the Medicare Nightmare on Alison's life and the fact Alison was a normal healthy young female who fell into the trap of the Medicare Nightmare overnight, her story will be used as a main reference case-study in this book to help exemplify how healthy individuals can find their lives easily turned**

upside down through failing to access appropriate medical treatments and professionals in a timely manner. The health issue presented in this case study is less important than the crucial lessons it teaches us about our health system and valuable insight given as to where our health system can potentially fail individuals.

Stage Five of the Medicare Nightmare:

Mary sought medical treatment over several years to help her overcome chronic back pain caused by having several slipped discs in her spine which was destroying the quality of her life. Mary was unable to be treated as a private patient due to her poor financial situation and instead went on a public waiting list to perform her spinal surgery. During the surgery, the registrar cut a nerve in Mary's spine which caused a degenerative loss in control over her muscles. The surgeon dismissed responsibility for the timing of the progressive nerve damage and stated to Mary that she must have already 'had it in her system' even though Mary did not suffer from such complications prior to the surgery. Mary became disabled, progressively losing her speech, balance and control of her limbs, needing her daughter to leave her employment for several years to be her carer. All aspects of the Medicare Nightmare were strongly manifested and her suffering was very observable to the outside observer. Her situation was irreversible and lead to her premature death at the age of 54.

While, the experience of the Medicare Nightmare varies along the continuum with increasing suffering as we move from left to right of the continuum; on the national scale, the effects of the Medicare Nightmare are mainly felt on a financial level due to the impact of having people inefficiently return to the health system to seek treatment, take continuous sick-leave or seek government assistance due to being unfit for work. Our welfare system is forced to pay up with more Australians exceeding their sick leave benefits and becoming unfit to work due to predominantly preventable health problems. They suddenly have a legitimate reason to not look for work or work less and receive government benefits. Our tax system is also forced to mop up the mistakes of the healthcare system. Sick individuals work less- less work means less tax is paid, leading to a reduction in national taxable revenue with a negative carry over effect on improving our national future infrastructure and living standards.

The Australian Governments increase of the Medicare levy by 0.5 per cent up to 2% to fund the National Disability Insurance Scheme in July 2014, while attempting to address the needs of the 400,000 disabled Australians needing carers, also merely dealt with the symptomatic effects of the poor information flow in the healthcare system which has led to increasing disabilities or permanent health conditions which impair individuals ability for self-care. As this book will argue, there are many victims who should never have been diagnosed with a disability in the first place, as their loss of health and mobility could have been easily preventable, had they had timely access to valuable information. The disability tax, while increasing the necessary funding for the disability scheme is somewhat reactionary and forces many Australians to pay for the inefficiency of our healthcare system and the consequential increasing disabilities in our society- many of which are preventable in the first place.

However, as will be seen in later chapters, this poor access to information flow in our society dooms us to having more individual Medicare Nightmares and exacerbates the Medicare Nightmare faced collectively by our nation as a whole, leading to a threat to Medicare's very existence. Part of the problem is the erroneous analysis and perception of our health system as a separate system rather than a complex system that is interlinked with other government systems such as education, welfare and tax. For example, education as will be seen later plays a crucial role in educating others to make more effective medical decisions, whether it be for themselves or others. Thus, unless we view the Australian healthcare system as part of a broader network of systems, we will fail to recognise the real costs inflicted on our society through poor medical decisions and outcomes.

Unlike medical negligence, the Medicare Nightmare is not just concerned with the errors medical professionals make, but rather the contributing causes to those errors and how poor information flow in our society -both within and outside of the healthcare system dooms many of us to make inadequate health decisions with often disastrous consequences for both the patient and the government systems involved. Medical negligence can destroy lives as much as workplace negligence, despite this, little if any compensation is available when medical professionals make erroneous decisions about patients' health and destroy their lives. Instead, patients are forced to suffer and bear it out, dragging their loved ones and families through the mud with them with Medicare once again forced to mop up the cost. The longer these trends continue, the harder it will be for Medicare to keep up with the rising costs in healthcare meaning that if the inefficiency of our healthcare system is not addressed, the inevitable outcome will be more personal medical errors and expenses and less health rebates for all. This will also further increase the costs of having private health insurance, making private health insurance inevitably accessible to only a small privileged segment of our society in the future due to the increase in claims poor health choices lead to. The end outcome is a sick society with many Australians quality of life destroyed and national GDP negatively affected.

The injustice lies in the fact that the onus is on the patient to find the right medical information and the right health professional at the right time to make the best decisions for their health *despite* being placed in a health system plagued with a lack of choice and poor access to *vital* information.

Offering free Medicare services, while yet limiting health consumers access to information that allows patients to make adequate decisions regarding their health only spells a disastrous, unsustainable health system and future hardship for all when the Medicare system continues to pull back rebates and support as it struggles to cope with a rising elderly population and increasing Medicare claims due to inadequate health decisions being made in the general population.

Some critics might use this as an excuse to suggest scrapping Medicare altogether, however the problem is not the free healthcare services but rather the inefficiency that plagues the health system as a whole and threatens the sustainability of the Medicare services we take for granted.

There have been varying figures or statistics (both legal cases and numbers) on Australians harmed by medical errors. The Medical Error Action Group of Australia (2013) estimates that **between 18,000 and 54,000 Australians are killed by their health care each year and**

that real figures are actually hard to access due to there
being no systematic collection of data and linking treatment
error data or even recognition of medical error as a cause of
death by the Australian Bureau of Statistics.

The Australian Patient Safety Foundation, a non-profit
independent research organisation concerned with the
improvement of patient safety, conducted research and
found that **at least 10% of hospital admissions are due
to potentially preventable adverse events leading to
as many as 50,000 permanent disabilities and 10,000
deaths each year in Australia.** If deaths from medication
errors are added, this figure doubles suggesting that 1 in
every 5 Australian deaths will be either from a medical
or medication error. They claim these figures suggest that
being a patient in an Australian acute care hospital means
that one has a 40-fold greater risk of dying from the care
received than from dying from a traffic accident, and a
400-fold greater risk of dying than working in the chemical
industry. **Iatrogenic injury (defined as unintended or
unnecessary harm or suffering arising from any aspect
of healthcare management) costs our health system
$2 billion per year with a potentially double cost in
total life-time cost of such preventable injury resulting
in high human costs for both patients and other
stakeholders. Medical misadventure also accounts for
more than 50% spent on compensation and insurance
by Australian State Treasury Departments** (Runciman
and Moller 2001).

**Comparing hospitals, public hospitals have more
than double preventable hospitalizations with lower
socioeconomic areas also suffering from almost double
the number of preventable hospitalizations than higher**

socioeconomic areas (AIHW 2013).

Approximately 190,000 people are admitted to hospital in Australia due to incidents with medication each year costing Australia annually **$660 million. Australia also spends close to 10% of its GDP per year on health care or AUD$4874 per capita** (Hunnam 2010) with healthcare expenditure rising faster than CPI **(ABS 2010).** By 2030, this GDP expenditure per capita is expected to double.

The number of people over 65 requiring healthcare services is estimated to double by 2030 and combined with Australia's current healthcare workforce shortage; efficiency in our healthcare system becomes more imperative than ever. Such reforms will ideally move our system away from an incident-based approach towards a more holistic approach that avoids preventable epidemic health crises.

As will be seen in later chapters, if only 2% of healthcare expenditure is spent on prevention and promotion and 98 percent spent on treatment, then more needs to be done not just within the healthcare system but society as a whole to educate healthcare consumers to make wiser choices regarding their most important asset- their health. Although more Australians are becoming progressively proactive in taking personal responsibility for the management of their personal health, they face many constraints when trying to find appropriate timely information and often despite personal initiatives, still end up making disastrous health decisions.

Furthermore, what is staggering is not that lawyers win over 95% of their medical negligence cases but that they reject over 90% of all medical negligence cases from

patients. Their rejection of such a significant number of cases though is not due to the cases not having merit but due to constraints in the legal system that make it difficult for patients to sue and be adequately compensated once they have been mistreated. Another significant concern however, is that 90% of people seeking the aid of lawyers feel that their medical professional failed to provide a reasonable duty of care and fulfill their responsibility when managing them. This translates to a large proportion of unsatisfied health consumers who feel let down by the very system they are forced to rely on when negligently treated. Unfortunately, the real human cost has been lost in the statistics with many patients essential feedback on their poor experiences with health services not captured by statistics or even the practitioners and hospitals that cause their losses.

Thus, there are many compounding, leading factors that contribute to an individuals' personal health crisis. It is confounding how individuals can be susceptible to potentially unlimited despair by being vulnerable, uninformed and disempowered when dealing with such a complex inefficient system. As the Australian healthcare system rarely acknowledges or apologizes to those whose lives it has destroyed, it is essential for all stakeholders involved including patients, to be more aware of how the Medicare Nightmare can be easily manifested- or avoided both on an individual level and on a national level as well. It is also essential for health consumers to learn to become confident health advocates for both themselves and their dependants to help counteract the power imbalance they will inevitably confront when seeking adequate healthcare solutions. This means that an understanding of all the intricate, risk factors which potentially lead to this tragedy becomes crucial, as will be demonstrated in the following chapters.

Chapter Two: Who is at risk?

There are many contributing risk factors which increase the likelihood that an individual will experience some stage of the Medicare Nightmare. It is crucial to be informed if one is at risk of the Medicare Nightmare to be able to decrease the likelihood that it may happen to them. This awareness is especially essential not just to protect one's health and wellbeing, but due to the legal limitations that victims of the Medicare Nightmare face once inflicted. These legal limitations occur due to patients being burdened with providing evidence in court to establish that not only a medical professional breached their duty of care by failing to provide them with a reasonable duty of care, but that the cause of their loss and suffering was due to this failure. As patients also usually have underlying or pre-existing health conditions, such proof is often difficult to provide as medical professionals can always counter argue that regardless of how they had acted, their patients' outcomes would not have been better due to their categorisation as a high risk case. This is a quite frightening scenario as it means that even if a medical professional neglects you after you have invested your full trust in their advice, you can easily find yourself disempowered if they do not put your interests first.

Therefore, some form of a basic checklist becomes essential to use as a tool to give one an idea of how much they are at risk of being a victim of the Medicare Nightmare. Individuals can use this useful checklist as a general guide and then take the necessary precautions to protect themselves from a prolonged nightmare. Explanations on why these risk factors have been selected are given at the end of the checklist to allow greater comprehension of the risks. The more boxes one ticks, the more at risk they are of falling into the trap of the Medicare Nightmare. Even if one ticks no boxes, they still must question if there are any other external or internal factors that put them at risk of the Medicare Nightmare as all cases of the Medicare Nightmare are unique and while cases of the Medicare Nightmare can be reduced through greater public awareness, it is incredibly difficult to prevent zero cases of the Medicare Nightmare from arising as the very nature of medical care always requires some form of risk taking. While eliminating risk may thus be impossible, mitigating risk *is* possible.

Medicare Nightmare Risk Assessment Checklist

1) Do you suffer from a complex health problem that is difficult to comprehend, treat or rare in occurrence but however demands almost immediate attention?

2) Do you suffer from continuous unstable income and employment or have you suffered from unstable income and unemployment lasting for a period of 6 months or more within a few years of seeking medical treatment?

3) Do you come from an ethnic or minority group with a Non-English Speaking Background (NESB) or indigenous background?

4) Do you have poor knowledge of how the healthcare system operates in Australia?

5) Do you have an overworked lifestyle with insufficient time to dedicate to making proper and careful decisions for your own personal health or the health of a dependent?

6) Are you a female at a child-bearing age either trying to conceive or at risk of having an unwanted pregnancy?

7) Do you live in a non-affluent suburb in the city or outside of a major city?

8) Do you suffer from a high stress level that impedes clear thinking when needed to face challenges in your life?

9) Have you struggled or do you think you might struggle in the future to locate a reliable and effective local medical professional when needed, if inflicted with any health crisis?

10) Have you recently been told by at least one specialist that you have 'no chance' or 'limited chances' to recover from a pre-existing serious condition?

It is important to note that these listed 10 general risk factors are not meant to be exhaustive in any way but simply serve as indicators that one is at risk of making inadequate and often regretful decisions about their personal health or the health of a dependent. The reasons these risk factors have been selected are discussed below as the more one is informed about why certain factors put them at risk, the more they are empowered to minimise those risks and make informed decisions regarding their health and ultimate wellbeing.

Risks factors assessed and explained

1) Suffering from a complex health problem that is

difficult to comprehend, treat or rare in occurrence but however demands almost immediate attention

The more complex a health problem, the more diligence and attention one must pay to who treats them, including how and where they get treated due to having a higher risk of being misdiagnosed and even mistreated. For example, some health problems like certain cancers such as Myxoid Liposarcoma's and injuries to a women's reproductive system such as Asherman's Syndrome (adhesions in the uterine cavity caused by trauma to the uterus) are difficult to diagnose and even treat. These conditions if left untreated for a long period of time can become incurable with more ghastly side effects and consequences. The proactivity of the patient becomes crucial here as they must cautiously deal with medical professionals who may easily dismiss their case and treat them as just another number. For example, despite Alison in case study four performing an intermediate level of research on Asherman's Syndrome, she still struggled to find appropriate medical professionals to treat her due to the rareness of her condition. Instead of curing her Asherman's, surgeons inflicted her with a second serious condition which was just as difficult to treat, doubling the number of future miscarriages and suffering that she would need to endure. It was very difficult in her case to find the right medical professional especially as the health system provides very little information on the individual success rate of surgeons. Indeed, she found that many medical professionals who were referred to as 'experts' in their field were far from experts where their surgical skills were concerned leading to them not just failing to cure her condition but exacerbating it instead, creating further future complications. Alison found that some medical professionals were also misinformed on what Asherman's Syndrome actually was and despite her efforts to provide them with relevant information, she still often suffered from their medical negligence. In the case of rare cancers such as Myxoid Liposarcomas, physicians often can overlook the swelling in a cancerous area and treat it as just another infection leading to further growth of cancerous cells and terminal outcomes. Other conditions such as a herniated or slipped disc in the spine might be more common in the general population, but incredibly difficult and dangerous to treat, thus requiring more skilled hands due to the significant surgical risks involved.

2) Suffering from continuous unstable income and employment lasting for a period of 6 months or more within a few years of seeking medical treatment

While being rich does not mean that one is immune from the Medicare Nightmare, it certainly helps in the area of prevention as one is less likely to find themselves in a position where they need to allow unskilled hands to operate on them. The tax system also offers tax incentives where individuals can avoid paying the Medicare levy surcharge if they invest in private health insurance encouraging them to make somewhat safer decisions for themselves. Unfortunately, financial strains caused by high living costs and unstable employment can force many people to reduce their healthcare spending and settle for less. Even if a phase of unstable unemployment has passed, the rippling effects continue to be felt. In a country such as Australia, where there has been an increasing trend towards the casualization of the workforce, the resulting job insecurity faced especially by those from minority groups or unskilled occupations has forced many to put their more urgent living expenses ahead of investing in preventative health care or even paying for adequate healthcare. This leads to both short-sighted planning and thinking which can be problematic because effectively managing one's personal health requires long-term strategic thinking and planning in order to avoid future catastrophes. Guardians and caregivers are likely to be hardest hit in such situations as they may be pressured to put the needs of their dependants before themselves and risk neglecting their own health. Ironically, it can be this sacrificial thinking that ends up harming the family unit in the end more than simply limited financial resources. Medical expenses also tend to pop up when one least expects it, making the 'inconvenience' of the timing of the health condition incredibly more harmful for the sufferer. This can lead to the future detriment of a whole family units' future, especially if one has just bought their first overpriced home in a city such as Sydney and is heavily in debt. In such circumstances, borrowing more is not a simple option or always possible.

3) Coming from an ethnic or minority group with a Non-English Speaking Background (NESB) or indigenous background

Australians from NESB tend to be less familiar with the complex healthcare system that they must deal with and the range of treatment options available to them leading to more risk taking when seeking medical treatment and ultimately more errors. As will be seen, sometimes racial or ethno religious differences can also impact on the quality of treatment one receives in the Australian healthcare system. Indigenous Australians also suffer from poorer health outcomes than non-indigenous Australians. According to Kelaher et al (1999a), indigenous Australians face many practical barriers to healthcare including child care, transport, service hours, cost and lack of information. For example, indigenous women may find it difficult to attend health care services due to a lack of access to child care services and transport. In the last few decades, the major causes of morbidity amongst indigenous Australians have been heart disease, diabetes mellitus type II, infectious diseases such as diarrhoea and respiratory infections- most of which are preventable. Indigenous Australians are also more likely than other Australians to be hospitalized or stay longer in hospital. Thus, minority groups within Australia can face substantial barriers when trying to access adequate healthcare.

4) Having poor knowledge of how the healthcare system operates in Australia

The healthcare system within Australia can be quite complex where treatment and insurance options are concerned. While public patients including emergency victims often do not have a choice regarding the location they are treated, private patients obviously have more choices. The public hospital system is also mainly staffed by registrars who are managed by a consultant from a distance, in contrast to the private sector which is mainly staffed by consultants. However, the distinction between the two is not quite clear cut. Medical specialists in the private sector can sometimes refer a patient to a specialised public hospital if they feel that they are dealing with a unique or difficult case and vice-versa. Thus, there is some element of collaboration occurring between public and private health services. Sometimes, experts in a particular field work in private practice- at other times experts may leave their private practice either partially or completely for some high ranking position within the public health system depending on their field. Within the public health system, there is also a hierarchy of professionals that one must pass through in order to access an experienced medical specialist, in contrast to the private system where one expensively 'shops' for the right specialist until they finally find someone that can adequately meet their needs. Understanding the hierarchy of employees within hospital systems is essential for knowing when to escalate matters, switch between public and private patient status and for comprehending ones rights as a patient.

Furthermore, as the Australian health system also offers different rebates for different services, this heavily impacts on which services are affordable and which are not. There are many issues to consider when interacting with the healthcare system and the more knowledge one has, the better they are in a position to make appropriate decisions regarding their health and the more control they have over their health outcomes. Of course, the opposite also applies; the less knowledge one has about their healthcare system, the less they are in a position to make appropriate decisions regarding their health and the less control they have over their health outcomes, ultimately leading to some stage of the Medicare Nightmare. Indeed, the worst way to learn about the healthcare system is through an emergency situation which does not allow one to absorb and analyse information effectively often leading to disastrous outcomes. This may sound humorous, but in fact often occurs in some individual situations where patients gain most of their crucial information on the healthcare system after an emergency situation has occurred, resulting in a sharp realization that they know very little about who or what they are dealing with. Needless to say, disastrous decision-making regarding ones health often follows as a result.

5) Having an overworked lifestyle with insufficient time to dedicate to making proper and careful decisions for your own personal health or the health of a dependent?

It may sound obvious, but the more overworked one's lifestyle is and the less time they have to dedicate to solving and researching their health woes in order to make proper, careful decisions about their personal health or the health of a dependent, the more likely they are to fall into the trap of the Medicare Nightmare. An overworked lifestyle means that one is more likely to neglect their own health by not sacrificing sufficient time to create a personal health management plan leading to higher treatment risks. Sometimes, what is perceived to be a minor health issue can in fact be a major health challenge if one overlooks their symptoms. It is for this reason that each health problem one encounters should be analysed thoroughly and not lightly dismissed. One must be ready to sacrifice hours, days or even weeks to solve an impending or potential health crisis. This may sound logical but how many people are actually willing to take days or weeks off work to create an appropriate health management plan if needed? The more complex or multifaceted a health problem is, the more time one needs to dedicate to solving it. At times, this can become draining and make one feel overwhelmed by their health issues, encouraging them to 'let things go' and just 'see what happens.' Many individuals simply are not ready to drop their priorities to focus on their health and have their aspirations for their future compromised. Health challenges demand patience which is much easier in retrospect than trying to escape a Medicare Nightmare.

Needless to say, regardless how much time your health condition demands from you, stop, research and ask questions. Otherwise, you may reach a stage where regardless of how much time you invest to circumvent a health disaster, it may be too late if the damage becomes irreparable.

6) Being female at a childbearing age either trying to conceive or being at risk of having an unwanted pregnancy

One legal firm estimates that mistakes made in **obstetrics** and **gynaecology** account for over a half of all medical negligence compensation claims currently represented by solicitors in Australia. These are women who have not experienced the Medicare Nightmare but have sued medical professionals that have neglected them. Simply being at a reproductive age and trying to conceive puts one automatically at risk and how one chooses to mitigate that risk becomes an individual decision that must be made. With obstetrics, a woman is not just concerned about her own individual health but the health- or compromised health in the case of the Medicare Nightmare, of her unborn child. Many things can go wrong with obstetrics, withal, there are times when a safe decision is simple to make and at other times difficult due to the complexity of the situation. There are many women who regret their choice of obstetrician after it is too late and the loss is irreversible. Being at risk of having an unwanted pregnancy can also be a risk factor as routine procedures used to clear either an incomplete miscarriage or unwanted pregnancy such as dilate and curettage can sometimes carry unforeseen risks. Asherman's Syndrome and endometriosis can sometimes result from such procedures compromising the success and safety of future planned pregnancies. Some women unfortunately do not discriminate where they seek treatment to remove an incomplete miscarriage or abort a foetus, only later to find that their future ability to carry a healthy baby to term has been compromised. This is because the uterus, if damaged in any way can compromise the survivability and health of future children and lead to complications such as premature labour, posing serious health complications and risks for both the mother and the unborn baby forever. Unfortunately, as bionic wombs have yet to be utilised in the medical field, safeguarding the health of one's uterus is crucial if one has any future aspirations for motherhood.

7) Living in a non-affluent suburb in the city or outside of a major city

While most public hospitals are managed similarly, some have a reputation for safety better than others. Likewise, while private hospitals have a similar structure within their industry, some employ more skilled and specialised staff than others. Generally speaking, the more skilled medical professionals tend to cluster in specialised centres or hospital units in the more affluent, inner areas of major cities. This is mainly a concern if one suffers from a serious health condition and needs the 'best of the best' to treat them but limits themselves geographically when seeking medical treatment. Sometimes, health conditions can also impair an individual's mobility, making it very difficult to consider specialists further than 30km away from home. Mobility problems caused by knee injuries, back problems and difficult pregnancies may limit mobility by making it very painful and difficult to travel further away from home, thus pressuring one to settle for local services. Living near specialised hospitals is certainly advantageous when one needs access to good quality healthcare for complex medical problems. Being forced to rely on local health services on the other hand is not just potentially expensive but deadly as well. There is no guarantee of course that one will avoid the Medicare Nightmare by being treated in one private or public health setting instead of another, but it is still clear that the better private and public hospitals are located in the more affluent areas of major cities such as Sydney.

8) Suffering from a high stress level that impedes clear thinking when needed to face challenges in your life

As an overworked lifestyle limits the time one has to dedicate to solving an existing health concern, stress is the main inhibitor to clear thinking and finding optimum solutions. It is also stress that convinces one to 'throw in the towel' and settle for any solution rather than the best solution. Sometimes, health conditions alone can cloud an individual's judgement making it difficult for them to assess treatment solutions and panic instead of think clearly. Physiological symptoms such as a fast heart rate, high blood pressure or a high basal body temperature may exacerbate this. Pressure to make a fast decision in a limited timeframe can also force one to suspend researching into their health condition and simply follow the first referral or solution they encounter. Unless one can step back objectively and logically assess their situation, it is highly likely that they will select the wrong specialist or treatment plan and thus create their own unique version of the Medicare Nightmare. As health inflictions tend to arise when one is least prepared to deal with them or at the most inconvenient moments in an individual's life, stress levels that impede clear thinking present high risks for anyone hoping to make appropriate medical decisions in their life.

9) Struggling to locate a reliable and effective local medical professional when inflicted with a health crisis

It is very disheartening when one anticipates that their family general practitioner will give them the best referral possible, only to find out later that it was nothing but just a random referral. Although patients hope that they that have been sent to a specialist that understands their needs and condition, they may realise soon later that their search has been elusive when the professional fails to help them. Especially, if one has an uncommon health woe, it becomes even more challenging to acquire good referrals from friends and family. 'Medical professional shopping' becomes inevitable, exhausting and incredibly costly. For example, although Alison was reassured that a particular professor was a guru in his field and could cure her Asherman's by removing her adhesions, she became very disheartened when she found out that his surgical skills did not match his research credentials. He gave up on managing her case and it was only accidentally after she confronted his male ego by asking for a referral to seek a second opinion that she was able to stumble upon a competent surgeon. Unfortunately, despite the competence of this latter surgeon, the side effects from poorly treating the Asherman's Syndrome caught up with her later. It is very dumbfounding how uninformed surgeons may be about their peers' success rate with different surgeries in their field. It is even more disheartening when a lack of access to adequate surgeons leads to patients adopting a trial and error approach to finding effective specialists to treat them, increasing their risk of being enveloped by the Medicare Nightmare and imprisoned in a cycle of mistreatment and suffering. The human body is not a car; one cannot keep trying different surgeries to see what works in the hope of eventually finding the right 'fix-it' solution. The delicate human body can only endure so much and the *timing* of the cure or finding skilled specialists in a *timely* manner is crucial.

Unless one is an avid user of social technologies such as online discussion groups, support groups and forums, their chances of finding the right referral or specialist may become more limited if all physical contacts have failed. In retrospect, Alison realized later that had she had the confidence to navigate her way through online support groups in the beginning of her journey into the abyss, she may have had a greater chance of stumbling upon the most appropriate surgeon earlier and would have perhaps prevented the disastrous consequences of having unskilled surgeons operate on her.

10) Having recently already been told by at least one 'specialist' that you have 'no chance' or 'limited chances' to recover from a pre-existing serious condition

If you have recently been told by at least one specialist that you have 'no chance' or 'limited chances' of recovery from a serious condition, then chances are that you are about to embark on an experiment where you find yourself a guinea pig involved in a risky trial and error approach while trying to reclaim your health. This doesn't of course mean that you *do* have no chance of recovery and unless several specialists claim this, then you should just consider the comments as merely an individual's opinion.

The real concern with such comments is that they mean that you will most likely need to interview more expensive medical professionals, trial different surgeries and ultimately take more risks with your health. The significant risk here is that in the process of trialling new surgeries and surgeons, more medical errors and disasters are likely to occur and jeopardise the success of any future treatments. The words 'no chance' and 'limited chances' also may imply that your medical professional feels challenged and unsure of whether or not they can help you, perhaps even resorting to more experimental treatment approaches. Chances are that you also have a long road ahead of you where treatment is concerned as the longer one seeks treatment, the more likely it is that new health conditions emerge and further complicate the treatment process. Thus, chances are that once you hear these comments, the Medicare Nightmare has either already started or is about to begin.

Chapter Three: Women's oppression through the Medicare Nightmare

No one is more oppressed and suffers from the Medicare Nightmare more than women. This is because of our biological function and burden to carry children. As previously mentioned, more than 50% of medical negligence cases brought forward by lawyers are in the area of obstetrics, yet when this is added to women's suffering in other areas of health, takes the number of Medical negligence cases brought forth by women to be more than 70% of total cases. This does not include the numerous women (90%) who do not sue although they have suffered from a medical error inflicted on them. This is a huge concern as it reveals that women are not very confident and satisfied with the decisions they make about their bodies and often end up regretful. Losing control over one's body is the most disempowering experience for a woman.

Perhaps, the proliferating number of women committing to elective plastic surgery also suggests that women commit to elective surgeries more significantly than the male gender. Even beautified procedures such as plastic surgery can become a nightmare when performed under the wrong hands and ironically, the plastic surgery industry is one of the few stakeholders that actually benefit when mistakes are made on women's bodies in the healthcare industry. For example, the use of genital surgery such as labioplasty (which is increasingly being performed in Australia) to rectify damage caused to a woman's genitalia.

In an era of advanced healthcare and technologies, we are easily made to believe that we are safer in medical professionals' hands than ever before. Despite this, the costs of Medical errors in our society are proliferating. Modern concepts on sexuality, while liberating women to choose and challenging men who have historically practiced polygamous relationships have harmed women's bodies through naturalising the need to go under the scalpel in order to attain unreachable ideals of beauty and creating the allusion that should a woman accidentally find herself carrying an unwanted child, the procedure to remove an unborn child poses no harmful, long-term consequences or risks for the woman's womb.

I question the frequent and blind use of dilation and curettage (otherwise referred to as a D & C) procedures which rob many women of their fertility and while I value this procedure as a lifesaving procedure, I also question women's lack of knowledge about the different methods of carrying out this treatment- for D & C's can be carried out both blindly and using guided imaging. Different surgical instruments used to perform the same procedure also lead to different results and risks. It is essential that women have a more empowered understanding of the frequent procedures that they may undergo during their lives, in order to ask the right questions and avoid future regret. It is not just married women who need to be wary about D & C's after miscarriages but sexually active women as well. While motherhood may not mean much to a vibrant woman in her early 20's, it can become a central issue in her early 30's if her uterus has suffered damage through a carelessly performed D & C. The main concern here is when such routine hospital procedures cause future infertility issues. These fertility issues can take many years to resolve, making it difficult for women to receive consecutive care from the same specialists as within the timeframe they are treated, their providers may move location or retire, making timely and coherent decisions more difficult.

Indeed, this can be quite tragic as one woman I encountered reveals. I will refer to her as Cara for confidentiality reasons. A bubbly intelligent student, Cara fell pregnant from someone she thought cared about her. However, her boyfriend threatened to leave her if she didn't abort. Believing he was genuine about his affection, she had a general D & C performed. Less than a few weeks after her abortion, her boyfriend terminated their relationship anyway. As a result of the D & C, Cara suffered from endometriosis, a painful condition affecting her uterine lining that required ongoing surgery and treatment. Cara was a caring young woman with a bright career in front of her. She was not promiscuous in character but had just made a mistake of falling pregnant with the wrong person's child. While her ex-partner continues to enjoy his manhood to this day, Cara's confidence, health and fertility was shattered as she was informed that she would face great future hardship when trying to fall pregnant again. This would also jeopardize all future relationships with men. Ironically, fun or unprotected sex in the early 20's can cost a woman her unborn children in the future.

Increasing expectations of women to be both beautiful breadwinners and considerate carers also creates a 'Superwoman Syndrome', where women's roles and duties continue to inflate parallel to inflationary pressures in modern society. In their pressure to perform, women are required to adequately meet the needs of demanding family members, often neglecting themselves due to fears of failure or guilt. These women generally behave as superwomen do; they work most days of the week, are engaged in further personal development, their house is usually clean, their children are engaged in extra-curricular activities and succeeding at school and their spouses are fed most days home cooked meals. Such women- if they don't suffer from eventual burn-out, become particularly vulnerable to the Medicare Nightmare if inflicted with any serious health concern. If a woman's family members fail to be supportive and compensate for her loss in health, then her Medicare Nightmare is simply magnified further. She will also find herself facing a system with limited choices in certain obstetric surgeries if her reproductive system has been harmed such as trans-abdominal cerclages and operative hysteroscopies. Only a few surgeons have a success rate with trans-abdominal cerclages of more than 90% across Australia, with most of these surgeons near retirement age. Most actually practice a simpler form of treatment for the incompetent cervix condition called the McDonalds' Cerclage, despite the fact that many of these surgeons boast a success rate of less than 60%. This means that almost half the women having this surgery performed on them will go on to bury their baby rather than carry it or deliver their baby prematurely with long-term health complications and risks. Operative hysteroscopies also deserve special mention here as exemplified in Alison's case. Although, the hospital information sheet given to her for her hysteroscopy procedure referred to the associated risks as minor and rare, she ended up having two serious health issues as a result of the failed surgery; so rather than being cured for her first initial problem, she ended up needing ongoing future surgeries to solve two serious problems! Interesting enough, no one who produced the pamphlet or associated with the surgery ever bothered to contact her and ask her about her experiences and even had they done so, the real consequences would not have been apparent till at least 12 months down the track, where she realized that she had miscarried due to having an incompetent cervix caused by her prior poorly performed hysteroscopy. Such incorrect information continues to circulate in both private and public hospitals, misinforming women about the actual risks of procedures that they are committing to. Such pamphlets also do not educate women about the most important risk aspect of the surgery- the surgeon himself. Not all surgeons safely perform this procedure increasing the need for future repeated surgeries for some women. What is most frightening perhaps is that the people that perform these procedures are also often referred to as 'experts' in their field.

While Australian women are often misinformed about the risks associated with routine procedures carried out in hospitals and by their obstetricians, they also face a lack of choice not just with finding successful surgeons but with IVF medicines as well. For example, despite the fact that progesterone injections have been proven internationally to help maintain the sustainability of pregnancies and are available in most countries around the world including America, Europe and Eastern countries, they are not available in Australia. Instead progesterone pessaries, capsules and creams are only available, despite the fact that some studies have shown that injections are the most effective method to deliver progesterone fast to a pregnant woman's body to help sustain a pregnancy. Pessaries are also associated with a higher risk of infection and should such infections develop, may lead to miscarriages or premature births. My friend shared an amusing story with me of one such woman who did not want to take such risks and walked into her Sydney pharmacy to request progesterone injectables. She gasped when informed that they were not available in Australia and cried, 'Well, we have no problem accessing them in Africa!'

Feminists take note! Even if a woman is career oriented with raising children at the bottom of her list of priorities in her earlier years, she still must take her reproductive health very seriously or she may find her career easily undermined at a time when she should be at the prime of her career. Infertility treatments and troubled pregnancies send women out of the workforce faster than any government legislation or economic downturn can.

The significance of doctor-patient relations is crucial for women to consider before selecting medical professionals to manage their case. Sometimes, being a woman can be an impediment to having oneself heard by medical professionals, especially if the woman is from a minority background.

For example, had someone told Alison in her early 20's or her fiery feminist days that in a decade's time, most of her energy would be consumed with trying to have children, she would have probably ended her life at that moment. Her experiences with medical professionals both in the public and private sectors illustrate perfectly the oppression of women in our healthcare system. Her experiences did not just damage her health, but her career, self-esteem and even her marriage. Having had a normal pregnancy with no complications and being able to work until 9 months in one of Sydney's toughest schools, the most devastating medical error was made during an emergency caesarean at a public hospital to deliver Alison's first child. A second registrar instead of a consultant was sent to aid in her emergency delivery, only to perform what can only be described as a butcher's job of a caesarean. This led to an emergency D & C only three weeks later and inflicted her with a moderate to severe case of Asherman's Syndrome or uterine scarring. Alison was shocked when her local GP sent her to an obstetrician who was bluntly condescending, disrespectful and demeaned her opinions about the condition she thought she had and should be tested for. Needless to say, Alison became traumatised before she was even diagnosed and felt surprised that such a misogynist character could be referred to by his peers as an 'expert' in women's health. He did not bother explaining to her, the treatment options available or what she could do to get a quick diagnosis and instead offered to put her at the end of a long waiting list of 'priority' and paying patients. He even was abusive and shouted commands at her making her feel violated and humiliated when touching her body. Alison ended up changing not just her obstetrician but her GP too, as a result of her horrific experience. It took the healthcare system 8 months to confirm the condition she knew she already had from a simple Google search. Unfortunately, dealing with the male chauvinist ego would become a common experience for Alison for the next decade while navigating her way through this system.

The next 'expert' Alison was to encounter candidly invited a registrar to witness his gruelling news that the operative hysteroscopy she had to remove scar tissue from the Asherman's was not successful and that she had no chance of recovery or ever having any children. He even became offended and tried to avoid giving her a referral for a second opinion when she requested one. The 'expert' after that admitted to her that despite being referred to him for her first high risk pregnancy and

seeing him for two months, he still had not bothered to
read her referral letter and had no idea what Asherman's
Syndrome was but assumed it would 'clear up' by itself
during her pregnancy despite her concerns raised. He did
have time though to encourage her to pay out of pocket
for ultrasounds for the reassurance of her child's heartbeat
even though that itself was not a caution he really needed
to take. Needless to say, Alison immediately knew that
the pregnancy was doomed and miscarried less than two
weeks later delivering at home alone. It only gets worse.
After finding another obstetrician who appeared to be
kind and offer a listening ear, her concerns were again
swiftly dismissed about the effectiveness of a procedure the
surgeon had chosen to try to maintain her second high-risk
pregnancy. Alison was concerned that a more complex
type of surgery such as a Shirodkar would be needed due
to the timing of her earlier miscarriage. The obstetrician
disastrously insisted that despite his poor success rate for
his surgical procedure, it would still be effective in her
case and that he had experienced many complications
with the alternative surgery previously, such as excessive
bleeding on the operating table. He only considered shared
care, once it became clear that Alison would have another
second trimester loss. Regretfully, this further referral
had a success rate in the alternative procedure Alison was
enquiring about of 90% with minimal severe complications
for patients. The obstetrician informed Alison that once she
commenced 24 weeks which was only 3 days away, that
she would be transported to another hospital to have her
baby resuscitated in the specialised hospital's neonatal unit.

While visitors would comment on the great food and
beautiful views of Alison's private room as a private
patient, Alison was yearning to escape it as deep within

she knew that the private hospital was merely an early graveyard for her baby; she knew that as long as she was away from the high risk unit in the specialized public hospitals intensive care unit, that her baby would not be resuscitated. Three days away from the golden goal of 24 weeks, Alison delivered prematurely after her water broke. As the responsible obstetrician was conveniently away on a conference, Alison found herself in the hands of a new obstetrician she had never met before. He informed her that the law would not allow him to resuscitate her baby and that her baby had no hope of survival. Trying to convince her that her baby was already dead, he used a Doppler only to find a strong heartbeat. He nervously backed away and told her that ethically he could not remove her baby which had a strong heartbeat so he forced her to end the life of her baby and deliver her baby through medication, taunting her that if she did not agree, she would face a great personal risk of sepsis and other long-term consequences such as no more childbearing. He also coldly stated that he would not step in to help should her labour inflict further damage to her cervix. Thus, Alison was forced to murder the baby in her womb in a labour that cruelly took double as long as it should have, due to an error made during the delivery process which teared her cervix apart anyway. Alison lives in regret till this day, haunted and traumatised by the life she was forced to give up on. She was even convinced to perform an autopsy 'just in case' other factors were also involved due to the torturous delivery process squashing her babies features, adding to the guilt of not just murdering her baby within but cutting him up as well. Five years of hell in the health system and this was supposed to be Alison's reward for her perseverance. This was as close as Alison got to the golden halo. Both of her babies are currently buried in a Sydney cemetery just two rows apart. Indeed, Alison's battle with the health system to a large part had been a fight with the male ego. Even had Alison made it to the high risk unit to resuscitate her 23 week year old, her baby would have had a 50% chance of survival and a 50% chance of suffering from a lifetime of surgeries and disabilities. Alison did eventually meet competent obstetricians who did not suffer from the male ego and kindly offered her their expertise, but by then, it was too late. The damage had been done. Alison confides that she just wanted her foetus to have a chance to fight or breathe- not be murdered by the state after his mother had been traumatised and trapped in an abyss by the healthcare system.

Such is the price we women often pay when we are forced to reject our womanly intuition and blindly follow the advice of male medical professionals. Alison's intuition as a woman had always been strong in times of hardship as every time she would sense something was not right- her gut feeling would always be correct. Alison neglected this intuition, choosing the quasi-logic of surgeons instead- not because she lacked self-confidence as a woman, but because all of the males she was dealing with had titles such as 'professor' or some highly applauded position as a director on some obstetrics board across hospitals in Sydney. They were the top-shots in the field but still kept dismissing her concerns, thoughts and ideas, harming her in the process rather than healing her. Her life sounded like some horror version of Britney Spears 'Whoops! I did it again,' except that the obstetricians instead of acknowledging their errors and mistaken judgements would simply detach themselves and justify their errors with some other theory as to why things went wrong. Alison did wonder if her traumatising experiences and disadvantage were simply due to her just being a woman or being clearly from a minority group and therefore carrying some imaginary stamp on her forehead that somehow defied her intelligence in front of white medical professionals.

With more than five years of tertiary education, Alison knew her condition better than any of them and the hardest part for her to accept was that she was always right but still went against her intuition. This is because no matter how educated a man is, he will never truly know what a woman is experiencing within her body – he can only speculate and guess. *The scariest part is that the mistakes made on Alison have been made over and over again with other women with no accountability.* Through personal contacts, Alison discovered that the prestigious obstetrician she had been under the care of in the private IVF clinic had also insisted on the same disastrous procedure for a friend- only to have her miscarry twins- twice! As for the other well-known obstetrician who did not bother reading Alison's two-page referral letter, Alison did wonder if his other, mainly Caucasian patients, who walked out of his suite proudly close to term, had their referral letters read or not. Her suspicions were further raised after meeting a woman online from a similar ethnic background who claimed that this same Ob had purposely sterilised her as she had insisted that a procedure he pressured her to have would make her permanently infertile and it did! Regardless of what his motives were, Alison did offer him during her last consultation with him, a two page print out with the 3-4 conditions he needed to monitor for her Asherman's Syndrome highlighted from a 10 minute Google search. Yes, a 10 minute Google search by her Ob could have saved her baby's life. Needless to say, the Ob felt very embarrassed and flustered when the predominant reason for miscarriage was clearly highlighted as a risk of Asherman's, even though he had previously insisted it was not related at all and that she was just incredibly unlucky. Sadly, for every second trimester loss Alison had to endure, she had to also suffer two to three first trimester losses to even get there due to her Asherman's complicating her pregnancies with each loss requiring hospitalization, unpaid sick leave, further surgeries and destabilizing every aspect of her life.

The greatest challenge when dealing with the Australian healthcare system in many ways is facing the male ego and having your opinions as a woman respected and heard. Interestingly, women working in healthcare can harm female patients too by blindly supporting the patriarchal culture that pampers the male ego, creating even greater danger or risk for female patients. The same way that women can benefit each other through sisterly support and advice, they can also harm each other through undermining their opinions and supporting the male power structures that harm women's bodies in our society. Equally disempowering, Alison was also confronted by female nurses and personal assistants who would scoff and trivialise any questioning of their surgeons expertise or decision making with the net effect being that she would not follow her instincts. Men, regardless of their positions in society, do not have the right to dismiss women's opinions or intuition. Nevertheless, if a woman dares to question a male medical professional for any reason, she suddenly is made to feel foolish and paranoid when trying to make appropriate choices for her health. Being assertive when dealing with such intimidating characters in the health system becomes crucial if a woman is to have her medical needs met. This provides a strong example of why women need to be their own health advocates so that they feel confident enough to walk away from any male or female medical professional who does not respect their concerns. After feeling betrayed by the medical professionals Alison put her trust in, she is now much more vigilant about who treats her, how and where. Thus, there are more important things in life than avoiding offending the existing male ego in the medical profession, especially considering that excessive politeness and passiveness may result in burying one's baby. Unfortunately, as Alison's experiences would constantly prove, despite the existence of strong professional standards in the Australian medical profession, many medical professionals still fail to act in the best interests of their patients.

However, the oppression of women's bodies is not limited to just the health system. Should a woman find herself suddenly inflicted with infertility and unable to carry a pregnancy to full term she faces great legal challenges when dealing with surrogacy laws in Australia. Although within the last few years there has been a softening of the Surrogacy Act across Australia making it easier for parents to deal with daily matters such as enrolling their children in school, gaining birth certificates etc., women can find themselves not just at risk of hefty fines for commercial surrogacy but also unable to have their child legally recognised! While such laws were originally constructed to protect the exploitation of women in developing countries, they also punish women in developed countries such as Australia who have been unjustly stripped of their fertility. Thus, women can end up punished twice by the system and potentially criminalized when trying to overcome the injustice of being robbed of their fertility!

Surrogacy laws through prohibiting sex-selection in IVF can also punish women who have lost a baby from a particular gender and feel that their suffered loss from the resulting medical error or misjudgement is greater as a result. They were expecting to raise a girl/boy and had many dreams based around those expectations. It is ironic by Australian cultural standards that countries that have long been portrayed as being antagonistic towards women's rights such as Iran and India have more restorative surrogacy laws that benefit women who have been oppressed through damage to their fertility than Australia. This leads to many Australians choosing to have their surrogacy arrangements overseas- some to overcome barriers to their human rights; others simply who have given up on the Australian healthcare system altogether!

As women tend to seek medical products and services more than men, more needs to be done to educate them to make more informed choices. Poor decision making in obstetrics does not just cost women their fertility, but also jeopardizes their chances of carrying their unborn babies to full term, increasing their likelihood of having a child with a disability and the endless future stress associated with this task, while creating a liability for society in the process. The area of obstetrics deserves special mention and focus when debating the efficiency of our health system as it impacts on future generations of unborn Australians and is responsible for the majority of medical negligence cases. This is a huge concern as the effects of the Medicare Nightmare can be passed from generation to generation through disabilities and unhealthy offspring. The increasing number of women having children at a later age and experiencing infertility means that more careful decision making needs to occur long before a woman is emotionally ready for motherhood. Such futuristic planning is difficult to engage in, especially if women have limited access to information to help them make appropriate decisions about medical practitioners and the health system they deal with in the first place.

The area of obstetrics can easily lead to the oppression of women's bodies when medical professionals do not meet their patients' expectations or follow up when things go wrong to help prevent future mistakes to other patients. This leads to remorse for the victims of widely practised flawed procedures and more future suffering for other women who will later seek help. Nevertheless, big business and IVF services profit from women's losses and the trial and error approach taken with women's bodies, resulting in women paying a heavy personal cost and the government paying up again through Medicare.

It is not just the medical decision making involved that is questionable but how professionals approach women's bodies altogether in Western society. Comparing experiences of women's treatment by doctors both in Eastern countries and Western countries, one will find that in Eastern countries women feel that their bodies are more respectfully treated. This is because professionals in Eastern countries implement an element of shyness when touching a woman's body; they avoid looking or staring in routine procedures such as listening to a heartbeat and they tend to explain to a woman more carefully why they need to touch her body. When possible to increase a woman's comfort level, they will have a female nurse assist especially with simple procedures that require excessive or invasive touching of the female body. In contrast, the absence of such notions of shyness means that we often find male medical practitioners in the west approaching a woman's body as though she has somehow become his territory, making her feel violated and humiliated in the process of the treatment. This does not imply that all medical professionals in the West are like this, but it does imply that medical professional who have such a chauvinistic approach to women's bodies do not last as long in the medical field in the East or at least end up with fewer patients due to women's higher expectations regarding their treatment. It is this very basic notion of respecting a woman's body that must be considered in our society as one must question, if a male professional cannot even offer basic respect when dealing with a woman's body, then how can he have any hope of adequately medically treating her? Unfortunately, female sufferers of the MN often express a feeling that both their bodies and minds were not respected and instead violated during the treatment process.

Damaged fertility is not the only loss women suffer, as they face an increasingly casualized workforce with little sympathy for those who need any special treatment or extra time off work to sort out continuous health complications. It is easy for women caught up in the Medicare Nightmare to experience loss of full-time work and a restriction to casual or part time work which damages their prospects of being able to apply for future permanent positions due to their scattered work experience. Health conditions also often affect one's mobility- shattering a woman's confidence and self-esteem as reduced mobility often results in weight management issues.

Obstetrics is not just a concern for women though; when a woman's health deteriorates, the whole family is affected. Women who suffer from the Superwoman

Syndrome and men who want to start families need to take extra precautions to safeguard the future health of their unborn offspring. Being at the centre of most families, when women's health collapses, the whole family suffers especially when the mother must leave full-time employment as a bread winner due to health reasons. Women can suddenly find that not only their role as a breadwinner is affected, but their role as a carer too as they struggle to care for their existing children. Women from minority groups need to take extra precautions, not only due to sometimes facing more language barriers than other women but also if they are from a culture that promotes self-sacrificing attributes of women. For example, although indigenous women die of diseases of the genitourinary system almost 20 times more than non-Indigenous women, many indigenous women still fear that paying attention to their own health can be a cost to their family as it diverts time away from other responsibilities (Kelaher 1999a). Feeling guilty when prioritising ones health can often become a significant risk factor for such women.

Being proactive and vigilant in the management of one's personal health can help prevent individuals' future suffering including the destruction of their quality of life. This becomes especially significant when a woman is confronted with a significant or rare health condition that seems difficult to resolve. Being complacent when making health decisions can ultimately destroy a woman's life and transform her role from being a carer to requiring a carer. Such a loss of independence can truly shatter a woman's career goals, hopes and dreams. Perhaps, the ultimate form of oppression of a woman is when she loses control over her body, especially simple womanly functions such as menstruation and childbirth, resulting in her having no control over whether she has no children or too many if she chooses certain routes of IVF.

IVF services deserve special mention here for as long as causes of miscarriage are not thoroughly or actively investigated by businesses specialising in IVF or surgeons unaware of best practices- especially surgical practices, women will continue to suffer and IVF businesses will profit at their expense. It is big business that profits with endless use of such services, harming those who rely on their expertise and put their trust in their professional judgement. Ironically, one finds that in the areas of obstetrics, IVF and gynaecology, although medical professionals may attend conferences on the latest developments in their field, many still lack knowledge about who the real gurus are in their field for different surgical procedures and conditions. The male ego in the medical profession becomes very blatantly obvious when male medical professionals, whether for financial gains or other, portray themselves as geniuses and avoid forwarding on their female patients to more effective hands when they need to. The complexity of seeking adequate healthcare means considering that even if an obstetrician gives you good advice in one area, he can still give you disastrous advice in another, leading to disastrous outcomes. Thus, the need for a woman to be her own health advocate cannot be underestimated.

Unresolved fertility issues for women can also be exacerbated once age becomes an additional factor, leading to more miscarriages which need further surgeries to resolve. The lack of support, women who suffer from recurrent miscarriage often receive in society only entrenches their existing pain and suffering. Despite the struggles a woman suffering from recurrent miscarriage experiences, after a third miscarriage, people assume she has somehow become 'used to' the losses, with some even cutting off their support. This casual attitude is predominantly due to the fact that many women suffer from miscarriages in society- approximately one third of all pregnancies end in a loss. However, not all women experience full recovery where they can finally have their children. Some are bedridden, require constant surgeries due to being unable to miscarry naturally, have their lives turned upside down in the process and still do not achieve their goal of having a baby in their arms. The pain of miscarriage in our society is severely underestimated as with every loss comes a loss of dreams and hopes, replaced by significant mourning instead. In the fight against such injustice, perhaps Alison used her body as a weapon but in the end paid the price heavily with her health, psychologically, spiritually and physically. Alison could not just put aside her 7 years of suffering and pain and just 'forget about it.' Justice to her became about restoring what was stolen from her in the first place. Experiencing medical professionals' negligence constantly and then burying babies as a result unnecessarily reveal that the psychological impact of the MN on its victims cannot be underestimated.

Those caught up by the MN soon realise that justice is more important than the success of their medical treatments. The fight for justice suddenly became more important to Alison than having children. Women are unjustly treated when they find themselves disempowered and harmed by medical practices which do not deliver best outcomes, due to a lack of knowledge amongst medical professionals about their peers' expertise and success rates with various surgeries.

The need to restore justice in one's life also becomes more intense when one feels that their ethno-religious group contributed to their medical professionals' mistreatment of them.

So how do you know that you are experiencing the Medicare Nightmare? You know that you are experiencing the Medicare Nightmare when you realize that the doctor treating you could have easily made a better decision, had he made your health needs his priority; you know that you are experiencing the Medicare Nightmare when you become trapped in a cycle of mistreatment that is both expensive and devastating to all areas of your life simultaneously; you know that you are experiencing the Medicare Nightmare when you find that you have a preferred place to have cannulas inserted inside your arm. You know that you are experiencing the Medicare Nightmare when you feel trapped as you have no real confidence in your medical professional and financial strains are limiting your ability to shop for a better medical professional. The Medicare Nightmare is a forgotten tragedy in Australian society, with many victims (predominantly women) silently suffering and feeling oppressed by it, however unable to comprehend how they ended up so powerless and depressed in the first place.

Chapter Four: Inefficient information flow in the healthcare system

Inaccurate information given to patients regarding procedures by surgeons and hospitals is not the only obstacle healthcare consumers' face when trying to access accurate and crucial information on the best treatment options available. Despite statutory protection for apologies in some Australian states (NSW and ACT), there is no complementary statutory duty to disclose adverse events in Australia with accident compensation placing the burden of errors on individual practitioners and not on the system itself in which they function (Shirley and Cockburn 2010). This means that medical practitioners in Australia are unlikely to disclose damaging statistics on the failure of their surgeries.

Such information access regarding surgeons' success rates is crucial as the position and title 'professor' does not necessarily mean that the medical professional is an expert in surgery nor does it guarantee successful results. Certainly, they may be familiar with the theories and research behind the conditions that they specialize in well, but it takes more than just education to make one a great surgeon in any field. A successful surgeons hand is a natural gift that one can somewhat develop through experience to a limited extent, but similar to natural flair, the surgeon either has the skill and capacity to heal or he does not. Having someone whose surgical success is limited or less than 70% performing on your body can be just as harmful as having an inexperienced registrar attempt the same operation. This is because despite the prominence of the commonly present egocentric attitude in the medical profession that often claims otherwise, medical professionals cannot be experts in everything they do. Some seem to stretch out their claims to cover being an expert in research and surgery with several flashy titles to woo the patient; yet logic tells you that there are only 5-6 possible working days in a week and more time spent perfecting one area of expertise means less time perfecting another. The jack-of-all-trades medical professional should ring a clear warning bell for patients to be cautious and encourage them to ensure questions on surgical success rates and risks are answered thoroughly and not simply dismissed. Specialists who claim to be leading experts in research and surgery along with a long list of board commitments spread across hospitals and medical organisations can also often mislead patients about their specific expectations.

Compare being a surgeon to being a teacher. The more one specialises as a teacher in any subject area, the more familiar, effective and confident they will be in that subject area. Alternatively, the more one stretches out their teaching expertise to try to teach many different disciplines, the less effective, confident and familiar they will be across all of the different subject areas. Now, consider the analogy of being a Science teacher; the more I focus on biology, the less chance I have of being equally effective in teaching chemistry and physics. Even if I am familiar with my subject area, biology, being involved in too many extra-curricular activities and wearing many hats that distract me from being in the classroom also means that I am less likely to be an effective biology teacher. Moreover, even if I was to be an effective biology teacher, regardless how confident I am with performing lab work, my practical skills will still most likely not match someone specialising in physical laboratory research. Similarly, as practice makes perfect most skills, in the medical field, if I do not perform a type of surgery often as a surgeon, my surgical skills will also suffer in that area. For example, even though many specialists will wear the title of 'surgical oncologist,' it does not mean that they are all capable of treating all forms of cancer. Some will be more experienced and skilled in treating and operating on specific parts of the body more than others.

Similarly, some obstetricians and gynaecologists' perform certain types of surgeries better than others. However, such information is difficult to ascertain before expensively outlaying a small fortune on specialist consultations forcing patients to adopt the 'shop for a doc' attitude as secretaries rarely reveal sensitive information regarding the specialists' statistics. This means that one must pay hundreds of dollars to access basic information on every medical professional they consider such as the number of times they have performed a specific procedure over the last few years and their success rate in that procedure. Of course, Medicare forks up the money too, paying for the disclosure of simple facts along with the patient. Some secretaries are even unable to provide simple information over the phone such as if their specialist performs certain diagnostic procedures or not! Although secretaries cannot offer diagnostic advice over the phone, surely such simple information on facts and figures must be more easily and economically accessible for patients?

Although Alison did eventually meet a 'professor' who was able to successfully remove the adhesions caused by her

Asherman's, he did not have an excessive list of affiliations such as being a director of obstetrics on medical boards nor did he pretend to be a jack of all trades and humbly would answer 'I don't know' when unsure of answering her questions. He also would kindly and voluntarily offer her a referral to see other specialists for issues outside of his expertise. His mannerisms as well as surgical skills made him trustworthy, professional and the ideal surgeon in all respects for Alison. A sign of his impressive surgery success rate was his international reputation which had women both cooing over him on online discussion forums and visiting him from all over Australasia. Trained overseas in Belgium, most of his Australian patients believe that his relocation to Australia was a pure blessing. In contrast, it is not a patient's perceived quality of care that leads to litigation but the perception that the treating physician was not honest and did not listen to their patients' needs (Shirley and Cockburn, 2010). Thus, the importance of a medical professional's character cannot be emphasised enough.

Regardless how skilled a surgeon is, a woman should never hesitate to question and actively engage in the decision making process for her health. Such confidence though ideally is present before one finds themselves deeply trapped in the Medicare Nightmare, where even the best decisions and surgeons will have minimal chances of restoring one's health.

The more complex a health condition is, the more crucial it becomes for a patient to have the most skilled medical professionals participating in collaborative care. It is thus not always about finding the 'magical professional' but sometimes the most effective team of professionals or specialists who can and are willing to collaborate effectively and share information and decision making. *Effective* care also means that knowledge about the strengths and weaknesses of one's peers in the medical profession is crucial. The Medicare Nightmare can easily become an eternal abyss if one is not connected to the right medical professionals in a timely manner.

Surprisingly, many specialists are *not* familiar with the comparative success rates of their peers for specific surgeries, meaning that although the specialist you are seeing might know someone who would more effectively manage your case, they may still be unlikely to forward you on to them. Although, most medical specialists attend several conferences a year on the latest developments in their field, they do not always have opportunities to compare personal statistics with their peers who perform similar surgeries, making comparison of medical notes, especially success rates for various surgeries somewhat rare or merely coincidental. Health conferences and seminars that focus on theory rather than practice and fail to maximise professional networking opportunities and lead to better patient outcomes, are not just simply a waste of time but can actually jeopardise the care patients receive. This occurs when patients pay for specific private services only to have their preferred surgeon managing their case abandon them during an emergency situation when they need them most in order to attend some random conference, and substitute in their place someone less experienced that either performs a poorer job or potentially exacerbates their patients Medicare Nightmare further due to a lack of adequate patient knowledge.

Lack of knowledge and awareness about holistic medicine can also be an issue if the medical practitioner or specialist does not keep up with the vast array of medical options available to patients. As many health consumers are increasingly selecting the more expensive and holistic path of alternative medicine in Australia, being aware of alternative treatment options available and their associated risks, herbal medicine contraindications etc. also becomes essential knowledge just as much as knowledge about modern Western treatments and medicines.

The proliferation of alternative medicine clinics in Australia is testimony to the fact that Australians have become more open towards holistic therapies over the last decade which offer beneficial holistic treatment for patients psychologically traumatised by their health condition or suffering from a vast array of complex conditions affecting several organs and systems simultaneously. Unlike western treatments which focus on the original source of the pain, alternative medicine treats not just the source, but many of the symptoms that arise as a consequence. Like many Australians, Alison also turned to holistic medicine when Western treatment had failed her. Although, she might have had faster results by taking hormonal drugs to improve her uterine lining, she became distrustful of a system full of side effects and was sick of feeling like a guinea pig, being also concerned about her overall health and wellbeing. For Alison, embracing holistic healing was a way to revalue and respect her body and allow herself to heal as a whole. It was expensive out of pocket as there were no Medicare rebates and her health insurance did not cover extras; however she found it restorative physically, mentally and psychologically. I am not advocating indiscriminate preference of holistic medicine over western medicine as both treat the human body from different perspectives and holistic medicine is more limited when

fixing structural problems with the human body; however
I am acknowledging the fact that eastern and western
treatments can generally complement each other and work
best together. Almost one third of the world's population
regularly uses traditional medicine when considering the
health systems of both China and India. In India, traditional
medical systems such as ayurveda, unani, siddha,
naturopathy, homeopathy, and yoga are well integrated into
the national healthcare system with traditional medicine
widely used (WHO 2001). In China, over 90% of hospitals
have an acupuncture clinic or units for traditional medicine
to help accelerate patient recovery. Surprisingly, in
Australia, the Chinese medicine profession on the other
hand has only recently joined the National Registration and
Accreditation Scheme for the Health Professions in July
2012 which is the same scheme that overseas accreditation
for other health professionals. Prior to this, the success of
Chinese herbal medicine was undermined in Australia due
to a lack of control over its supply and a lack of scientific
evidence to support its success; despite the fact that over
one billion healthy Chinese people worldwide presently
are physical testimonies to its historical success. While
the health systems of India and China have successfully
integrated their traditional medicine systems with western
allopathic medicine, the West has yet to exploit the
same benefits where using combined medical systems is
concerned. It also appears reluctant to acknowledge the
reality that patients in western countries are increasingly
turning to traditional medicine in the West for treatment
either out of curiosity or due to discontent with their
western medical systems.

In fact, many western practitioners advise their patients
to stay away from such alternative therapies due to a

perceived lack of empirical data, despite there being a strong movement and demand in the west for more holistic therapies that treat and target the human body as a whole. Numbers and statistics are thus often used to keep the status quo in the medical profession rather than inform and help educate patients to make more effective choices. Australians need more support to make more confident decisions regarding integrated health treatment plans including making decisions on Chinese Medicines whose foreign names do not provide any information or clues regarding their content, benefit and risks. Western medical practitioners must respond to the increasing demand of their patients for more holistic treatments and therapies that consider the role of the mind, body and soul of the individual in the healing process. The need for such holistic treatments is especially in demand by those seeking treatment for complex conditions such as cancer, infertility and ongoing back problems.

As patients, struggling to make effective medical decisions with limited information, we often find ourselves left entertaining our fears with Dr Google and our personal research skills which may or may not be adequately developed enough to save us. While online social forums provide useful information, they can also harm a patient just as much if the patient is unable to critically assess the information they stumble across. Today's avid and proactive health consumers engage with social technologies increasingly to communicate with others, research questions they have in order to help them make better health decisions and access suitable medical contacts. Many resort to such forums due to being unable to access health information relevant to their needs elsewhere, especially regarding medical specialists to enable them to make more confident decisions that they will not regret in the future.

The Australian government should encourage and assist online support groups which aim to help Australians access information on adequate treatments and link them to effective medical practitioners. Such support groups can help to significantly reduce the effects of the Medicare Nightmare on our society- or potentially prevent them altogether in some areas of health, while saving our healthcare system millions of dollars from poor medical decisions made by individuals and thousands of Australians from unnecessary personal loss and suffering. The feedback of a dozen patients online on a particular medical professional may give more insight on the medical professionals actual success rate than other referring professionals who may in fact, know little about the success rate and weaknesses of the professional they refer to.

Utilising the power of social technologies such as official online discussion forums, Skype and Facebook can help improve our healthcare system without the expensive outlay of government funds and resources as patients connect, compare medical notes and learn from each other's mistakes. However, some Australians have already taken on the initiative without receiving any assistance in the hope of helping others make better medical decisions- and avoid medical disasters! For example, the International Ashermans Syndrome Association operates a discussion forum where women all over the world discuss their experiences and frustrations with trying to find an adequate surgeon and treatment plan to help them overcome their infertility. The forum which operates as a Yahoo! group offers a database for members to list and compare medical notes and also a file on suitable surgeons divided up into A-listers, B-listers and C-listers with the first being surgeons who have received plenty of good feedback from patients and the latter being surgeons less well known with not many supporting statements regarding the effectiveness of their surgical skills. Women in the group actively support each other through making difficult decisions and avoiding medical nightmares with women participating all over the world from Africa to Greece. One Australian woman, Kylie Bolan, who suffered dramatically from Asherman's Syndrome began her own local Australian support group with the aim that her online forum would make it easier for Australian women to seek appropriate medical treatment in the Australian context and form helpful local friendship networks. Such individual initiatives have occurred with no outside funding or support, meaning online support groups must often resort to other means to raise the necessary funds to keep viable such as requesting regular member donations or selling T-shirts. Other significant initiatives of specific support groups include creating greater awareness on neglected and misunderstood conditions in society and amongst medical practitioners including surgeons while promoting prevention methods. For example, creating awareness through educating others about the unknown risks associated with certain procedures. Government recognition of such personal sacrifice can positively promote and support the enormous strength and initiative required by individuals to run support groups despite having endured tremendous suffering and loss themselves.

One must pose the question: Why must people learn the hard way? Why do dozens of patients have to suffer at the hands of an inept surgeon simply because they could not access simple details about their specialist that would have allowed them to compare their surgeon to other specialists and enabled them to make crucial decisions in their life regarding their health treatment? Why is no one in the healthcare system allocated the vital responsibility of monitoring unsuccessful surgeries performed by inept surgeons in order to discourage such surgeons from performing specific surgeries and instead forward their patients on to more skilled hands? As little compensation is offered by our legal system to compensate patients who have been harmed as a result of selecting the wrong surgeon, it only becomes natural and fair that with carrying the burden of responsibility for making poor medical decisions, patients should at least also have easier access to relevant information and figures regarding medical specialists and doctors to allow them to make more informed decisions in the first place. Such questions raise concern over the balance of power in the healthcare system with Medical professionals benefiting from the pervading lack of disclosure often to the detriment of patients.

It is cruelly ironic, that in a country such as Australia, with readily available access to all forms of technologies and the majority of its' population being privileged enough to own the latest communication devices, crucial information which can be easily disseminated and made readily available to patients online is instead restricted. Prevention using the dissemination of vital information through readily available technologies means that millions of dollars lost in the Medicare Nightmare can instead be saved through small investments which improve information access and overall information flow between all stakeholders in the health system. Thus, improving the efficiency of our healthcare system is not just simply about providing more beds, doctors and funding but about ensuring a more efficient overall allocation of resources that actually saves money through implementing precautionary measures and greater information awareness.

While political parties in Australia often centre healthcare discourse around whether to increase health funding or not, more sophisticated debates in the broader community need to take place that question what we are actually doing to mend the hole in Medicare spending caused by poor decision making by all stakeholders in the healthcare system.

The expanding population in Australia naturally means that more hospital beds, doctors, funding etc. will be needed, just as more schools and infrastructure will also be needed. The question thus should not simplistically focus on whether we need to spend more or not but whether we can more efficiently invest money and other limited resources to ensure better health outcomes for all. For decades, the access to healthcare argument has been trivialised and reduced to bickering about whether to fund the health system more/less ignoring the crucial elemental question 'how do we make our *existing* system deliver more *efficient* outcomes for all through a more *efficient* allocation of resources?' How can we gain more from every dollar that we spend in our healthcare system? Ironically, extreme cost-cutting measures usually mean that registrars are substituted for more skilled medical consultants in difficult procedures in public hospitals meaning that while money is saved in the short term, a fortune is lost in the long term due to the disastrous domino effects that occur. Errors made by registrars often signal that they are not confident enough with certain surgeries. Being overseen by a competent consultant to maximise training over a longer period of time would not just improve the skills of a registrar and prevent Medicare Nightmares for many patients, but also significantly reduce the burden on the constantly blown out budget for the health system. This is because while preventing a Medicare Nightmare can cost the health system one hour of a consultant's time, *not* preventing a Medicare Nightmare from occurring could cost the health system approximately up to one year's pay for a Medical consultant due to the patients' constant future hospitalizations and ongoing medical treatments! Thus, preventing just a few Stage 5 Medicare Nightmares per year may be enough to warrant supervision by a medical consultant for the more complex and risky surgeries in any public hospital for the same period of time!

Management staff within our hospitals who make crucial decisions regarding staffing are burdened with the difficult dilemma of trying to ensure satisfactory patient outcomes despite facing a constantly reduced budget for healthcare expenditure. Some hospitals seem to be a haven for Medicare Nightmares, with the responsibility for resulting disasters often attributed to the registrar, consultant or the uninformed patient, when the greater responsibility should lie with the overall inefficient healthcare system that is hampered by poor information flow between all crucial stakeholders, leading to inadequate decision making by all.

Other stakeholders include health insurance companies who usually own the private hospitals whose services their patients use. Some health insurance companies attempt to improve health outcomes and reduce their losses by administering questionnaires to their customers on their experience of the hospital service they have used and offer a prize for the most constructive responses. For example,

HCF sometimes sends short questionnaires to its members with some responses requiring an answer in a few hundred words to questions such as if one was a hospital CEO at the hospital they used, what initiatives would they take to improve the service standards at the hospital? Such simple feedback is crucial to owners and managers of hospitals both in the private and public health care systems to help them improve the efficiency of their services and reduce unnecessary costs which arise out of errors that occur. Unfortunately, insufficient feedback is usually gathered on the performance of most hospitals or surgeons with the added complication that sometimes the actual adverse effects of the surgery will not be apparent till at least 12 months down the track- which is way past the timing of most feedback collection. As medical professionals also feel stigmatised for revealing their medical errors, they also tend to underreport their errors meaning that the constructive feedback loop is often hampered and valuable information flow is obstructed.

When patients are rushed to emergency wards, immediate data collection must include whether the admittance has been due to a naturally occurring condition or a Medicare Nightmare. Case-studies of patients suffering from Medicare Nightmares can provide vital clues as to where our health system can fail and at what point's intervention and prevention are necessary. In the ideal scenario, information continuously circulates leading to key stakeholders such as hospital owners, health insurance companies and government bodies being actively informed about the trends in failure or success of individuals' medical decisions and taking corrective measures to improve the health systems efficiency within their scope. However, information is also continuously exchanged both within each sector and between health consumers, health insurance providers, government departments and medical professionals. Through improving the efficiency in information flow, money wasted in the Medicare Nightmare can be redirected into more constructive uses such as providing healthcare to an expanding population and meeting the challenges of an aging population which is crucial to Australia's' long-term prosperity and the sustainability of our health system.

Chapter Five: Education

From the day you are born, you are an immediate consumer of the Australian healthcare system- yet chances are you have never really been taught about effective decision making within this system and have just been 'expected' to make the right decisions in your adult years. You are just expected to manoeuvre your way through complex health problems, numerous complex options for health insurance and rely on health professionals for crucial advice. Ironically, you have also not been taught how to make the most important decisions in your life, regardless of whether you studied science, business or literacy- and regardless of what level you studied any particular discipline.

Being educated on avoiding the Medicare Nightmare is *not* about having a contingency plan for every possible health condition but about developing the necessary skills to analyse specific health information and ask the right questions when needed to make effective, timely medical decisions about one's personal healthcare- the same way one is taught and prepared to make decisions about ones' future career, education, family planning etc. It is about comprehending the complex details in our health system and the challenges one faces when dealing with medical professionals who wield significant power under state law due to protective measures which limit patients abilities to sue for damages and in the medical field, influence what medical treatments and medicines one can and cannot have access to. It is about being taught how to research possible support groups and find adequate health information should ones family, GP and surgeon be unable to aid them. It is about accessing knowledge which empowers one in an industry where they are more powerless in dealing with service providers than any other industry. While the material consumer who purchases faulty goods and services enjoys the luxury of knowing in Australia their goods or services will be replaced or refunded under the Fair Trading Act, the Health consumer is left to suffer from the consequences of the poor decision making of their service providers due to severe limitations imposed on them by the law to sue. They receive little if any compensation for their loss- which is considerably greater and has far more catastrophic implications for their life than buying a faulty DVD player or damaged item of clothing. Being educated on avoiding the Medicare Nightmare is about tipping the power balance back in favour of the health consumer, whose lack of power is entrenched by their lack of knowledge in dealing with the power imbalance that they often encounter in the health system. This information power imbalance combined with a financial power imbalance makes litigation against wealthy and well informed health care providers very difficult when things goes wrong- especially as it often does (Shirley and Cockburn 2010). Health care providers make mistakes whether from a professional or human angle just like any other profession but with more catastrophic losses and results. If knowledge means power, then the health consumer in Australia is surely the most powerless. Equipped with limited knowledge about dealing with a health system characterised by a power imbalance, being informed becomes crucial and easier access to quality information becomes a more just solution to help balance the effects of this power inequality.

Being educated on avoiding the Medicare Nightmare however does not just benefit the health consumer, but benefits medical professionals as well through encouraging them to become more informed about their peers work and therefore provide better advice and services to their patients, ultimately helping them avoid tedious lawsuits and patient injuries. It is ironic and a significant concern that even though some specialists attend conferences frequently and learn about new medical techniques and breakthroughs, they can still be unaware of the equivalent success rate of their peers for the same surgeries, meaning that more effective referrals are unlikely and patient outcomes are not maximised as a result. Better decisions on health treatment also benefits government as more effective decision making by both patients and their healthcare providers leads to a more efficient allocation of resources in health spending. It also reduces wastage in Medicare expenditure and improves society's overall wellbeing as a healthy society is always a more productive one.

Health education which will help individuals to make more effective decisions on their health and become confident health advocates for themselves and their families must at least begin in the early secondary years of high school where students are taught to analyse sources of information for their credibility and extend their research skills, before they venture off into higher education, vocational education or the workforce. Being able to utilise students' interests in social technologies and incorporate knowledge of these technologies with research skills on locating effective support groups, successful healthcare providers and asking critical questions regarding different health conditions, weighing up the pros and cons of different health insurance plans, treatments etc. will lead to learning essential life skills that impact on a student's life, much more than any other content from Science, Maths or English ever will. Being exposed to a real scenario analysis where students have an opportunity to consider themselves in the role of a patient making crucial decisions regarding their health or treatment is one possible context, such skills can be taught. It is necessary to burst the bubble of oblivion for youth, move students out of their comfort zone and force them to think about things they prefer not to in their naive teenage years. The attitude that 'such things could never happen to me' or 'I am too young to worry about my health' must be challenged as within a few years of finishing secondary education, students must accept adult responsibility for choosing and paying for their own health insurance and perhaps even making medical decisions about potential surgeries and treatment options. As many students eagerly save for a car in their early adult years, they should also be taught to save for a rainy day or keep aside emergency money should their health be compromised as they will face a workforce with increasingly reduced sick leave entitlements, increasing casualization and little mercy for those unable to commit to full time work contracts due to suffering from health complications. Ultimately, we are all responsible for improving the efficiency of our healthcare system and ensuring that we share valuable information or knowledge, through communicating success stories or our own version of the Medicare Nightmare with others to contribute to society's overall wellbeing.

The assumption that students will somehow 'know what to do when the time comes' significantly harms students in the long run and relinquishes the responsibility of schools to create informed and proactive citizens capable of self-autonomy as health conditions tend to strike with the worst timing not giving one time to think, research adequately or even plan ahead. If one is not equipped with the necessary skills to make informed decisions on their health in the present, then chances are that they will not have sufficient time to perfect these skills should a health challenge suddenly emerge. Furthermore, what could be easily dismissed as a trivial health concern may potentially become a future health disaster making proactivity and initial effective decision making even more crucial.

There are many ways that the education system can empower students to help them take greater ownership of their personal health.

Empowering lessons may include:

- Understanding medical jargon used in public and private hospitals

- Learning to carefully read clauses on surgery admission and consent forms

- Balancing and weighing the pros and cons of treatment options available

- Comparing different health insurance plans available and deciding which plan would be most suitable for different scenarios or needs

- Learning to ask doctors relevant questions using real case-study analysis

- Researching different support groups for information on a range of health conditions and their respective treatments

- Weighing up various health treatment plans on a tight budget

- Comparing the pros and cons of Eastern and Western medicine including holistic therapies such as acupressure and acupuncture

- Researching the structure and services present in overseas hospital systems such as in China and linking this to the increasing popularity and use of holistic therapies in Australia

- Brainstorming different ways to gather and evaluate referrals received from medical professionals, friends or other contacts

- Researching the strengths and weaknesses of the Australian healthcare system in which they are consumers and stakeholders in

- Researching preventative measures for serious common health conditions one will most probably encounter in their future such as diabetes, back problems, heart conditions etc.

- Considering one's personal genetic risks and using risk minimisation strategies

- Discussing the importance of one's health and wellbeing and why it impacts on every other aspect of an individual's life

- Comparing holistic therapies in terms of their benefits, costs and risks

- Learning about the importance of food and drug

safety using information from government health departments

- Knowing when to be suspicious of providers of both traditional and western medicines on offer (e.g. over prescription of antibiotics, non-disclosed herbs)

The discussion of different surgeries performed in obstetrics which can affect a woman's future fertility such as D & C's, caesareans and even 'harmless' hysteroscopies should also be incorporated into sex education for female students considering that they are just as crucial as learning about the various options available for contraception.

Sometimes having numerous choices can itself confuse patients especially if they must take immediate action regarding their health. Things they need to consider include: public or private insurance? Fully or part insured? Hospital cover, ancillaries or combined? Helping students to consider the full array of health insurance options available beforehand will make it easier for them to make appropriate decisions in a timely manner when needed. It is surprising how even highly educated individuals can still struggle with the details when it comes to selecting appropriate medical insurance cover or treatment plans for themselves or loved ones.

We can never guarantee ourselves that we will *never* fall into the Medicare Nightmare but we *can* reduce our chances of being trapped in it through having better access to pivotal information and improving our capacity to analyse medical dilemmas through developing our knowledge, awareness, problem solving and analytical skills. This will maximise our chances of making the best possible decisions for our health when the time comes.

Certainly, the Medicare Nightmare is the worst way to learn about the healthcare system as once you are trapped in it, you will learn how to make effective medical decisions the hard way. You will also be too traumatised by your losses and the impact it has on the quality of your life to the point you will find *any* decision making difficult- if not impossible. Technology savvy students will be relieved to be informed that access to having the latest mobile phone model with a reliable internet connection can be an invaluable asset when making crucial medical decisions in an isolated hospital room as it allows one to search for last minute information or old email contacts to facilitate fast decision making in emergency situations.

Although, there are no outcomes on learning about the Australian healthcare system in the new Australian curriculum for Science, the learning across the curriculum component addresses sustainability, personal and social capability and civics and citizenship. These contexts can easily incorporate education on our health system. For example, for sustainability, the Science Syllabus (BOS 2012) states that it 'provides students with opportunities to investigate relationships between systems and system components.' Expanding this concept to include studies on the sustainability of our health system and its interaction with other government systems, rather than just our ecosystem in an isolated context, would not only offer students a broader picture of the concept of systems, but it would also arm them with crucial knowledge about the most important system that they will ever deal with in their life. As the context of sustainability also explores relationships, cycles and cause and effect while aiming to develop students' analytical skills to allow them to examine relationships in their world and design solutions to identified sustainability problems, education on our health system would easily also complement this learning outcome.

Applying these concepts and skills to a study on our health system would empower many students to make more informed future decisions regarding their health and reduce their risk of suffering from medical errors that may cost them their life. The goal of the Science syllabus in making students personally and socially capable, aims to teach students how to manage themselves, their relationships and their lives more effectively. This includes establishing positive relationships, making responsible decisions, working effectively individually and in teams, in addition to constructively handling challenging situations. One key outcome is that students develop their 'scientific and technological understanding to make informed choices about issues that impact on their lives and consider how the use and application of science and technology meet a range of personal and social needs' (BOS 2012, p32-34). Incorporating content on our health system to achieve this outcome, allows students to directly consider the most critical area of their life that science and technology will ever impact on. The third most suitable goal which would lend itself to including education on our national healthcare system is the goal of civics and citizenship which 'involves knowledge and understanding of how our Australian society operates' (BOS 2012, p32-34). Ironically, students as yet have been given minimal information- if any on understanding how our health system operates. Assuming that students will learn broad skills and then one day magically be able to apply them to an incredibly complex health challenge with no clear solutions, creates significant future risks for students who can potentially

end up severely harmed by such a dangerous gap in
their education. More explicit teaching strategies which
incorporate ideas about managing health risks using limited
information and analysing treatment options would help
empower students to become healthier and more informed
citizens of tomorrow. Students should also be informed
that between 2 per cent and 3 per cent of all hospital
admissions in Australia are potentially medication related
(Roughead et al1998) and the dangers of self-medicating
oneself. Education becomes even more essential for those
from minority groups who may face language barriers
or discrimination when seeking health services, women
who must negotiate their right to make decisions for their
own bodies in a male dominated field and Indigenous
Australians who suffer from adverse child and maternal
outcomes, leading to higher rates of infant mortality due
to unawareness about the availability of health services
(Kelaher et al 1999b).

Other disciplines such as Physical activity and Sports
studies (PDHPE) can share the responsibility of developing
student understanding of the healthcare system in Australia.
For example, stage 5 outcomes aim to teach students to
'assess the individual, socio-cultural, political, economic
and environmental factors that influence health.' They
critically analyse how a range of health information,
services and products can be applied to meet specific health
needs. One goal is that students 'understand the uncertainty
of health information and how knowledge has changed,
and will continue to change' (BOS 2004, p52). Although it
does not directly deal with the crucial issue of making more
informed health choices in a complex healthcare system,
incorporating content or outcomes on understanding a
health system that will significantly impact on students'

future physical activities would allow these stage goals to be more fully realised. Whether students learn about the history of our health system, study the images in this book or even health advertising material for Module A (Distinctively Visual) in the senior English syllabus, there is room for disciplines other than Science to empower students to manage their most valuable asset- that is their health more effectively and thus contribute to society's overall wellbeing.

Even if being educated about our health system and how to make better medical decisions is treated as outside of the normal curriculum, such lessons can easily be integrated into school life using extracurricular workshops ideally that teach students how to avoid their own version of the Medicare Nightmare through skills based activities and discussions.

Ironically, having a higher education or even a Medical Science degree does not guarantee that one will not fall into the Medicare Nightmare as most tertiary degrees do not offer any education or insight into the Australian healthcare system, meaning that our education system as a whole fails to educate and empower individuals to be their own health advocates and make effective medical decisions in their lives. This results in many individuals not having the confidence to take responsibility for their own health and being totally dependant on a medical professional's judgement. While this by itself is still a choice, patients must beware that relinquishing responsibility can be risky once a consent form is signed or treatment avenue followed as the health system places the onus on the healthcare consumer to accept all risks, regardless of whether or not they have thoroughly read their consent form or researched the treatment option that they had consented to.

However, education is not just lacking for healthcare consumers but for medical professionals as well. Patients must feel more confident negotiating with their healthcare providers, their treatment options with more respect given for their concerns and wishes. A progressive change in the way medical professionals view their patients and deal with their concerns can help empower healthcare consumers to at least not regret the decisions they make- regardless of the outcomes! If the responsibility mainly falls on the healthcare consumers shoulders when things go wrong, it is only fair then that the healthcare consumer is educated enough to make more informed decisions and engage in a collaborative partnership with their healthcare providers and have their voice heard, rather than dismissed.

The best Australian surgeons Alison could find in terms of meeting professional standards with adequate surgical skills and considerate treatment of patients, were educated outside of Australia, suggesting that there is something missing in the education of medical professionals in Australia, such as effective surgical skills or the treatment of patients. As a healthcare consumer, part of her struggle was being heard and having her concerns respected by medical professionals. Indeed, had her health concerns been taken more seriously, her pain and suffering endured from the Medicare Nightmare would most likely have been significantly less. Such doctor-patient relations become more sensitive when gender power imbalances are considered; making active listening to patient concerns a must. This is because many women constantly find themselves struggling to assert their opinions and beliefs with male professionals who dominate the healthcare system and pressure them to make disastrous decisions for not just themselves but their unborn children as well.

Furthermore, in order to avoid liability, doctors and surgeons in Australia tend to employ a secular conservative way of communicating with patients. This is in contrast to countries for example, in the Middle East where patients suffering from critical or terminal conditions are told bad news mainly using euphemisms. At times, they do not even immediately receive the actual news about their diagnosis due to fears about it affecting their physical healing till further down the track when they are considered 'ready.' An example is the story of a woman suffering from a chronic cancer in a middle-eastern country. The woman was not informed that the surgeons had found an entire organ in her body plagued with cancer or even that the surgeons had removed this organ during her surgery. Only two family members were informed about the true nature of her condition with half of her children sensing something was wrong, but unaware of the root cause of their mothers' pain. The goal here was to help accelerate her physical healing as she suffered from intense chronic pain, with the belief that stress and negativity would only obstruct the healing process. Even when the woman was informed about her actual condition after she had healed from the surgery two months later, she was not overwhelmed with grim statistics about life expectations or the poor likely outcome of future treatment options available. Instead, she was given all of her information in a positive light, such as what to do about her condition, with the answer to all of her grim questions on recoverability being 'It's all in God's hands, just rely on God and God willing you will heal.' Such communication may be easily dismissed from a western perspective, especially as the word 'God' is rarely used in western medical settings. However, the woman healed relatively faster than expected and only suffered from mild depression due to her diagnosis. She also seemed to continue with her daily life normally, with her children often nagging her to slow down and work less!

Compare this to a family friend of mine who also unfortunately suffered from a terminal cancer in NSW. This person was told the news about their terminal case almost immediately, perhaps due to the surgeons' fears of future legal liability, with no apologies for sharing the bleak expectations on their short life expectancy, resulting in any hope of healing demolished. No euphemisms and no mention of God or hope here- only pessimistic worst case scenario outcomes. This person had a family of two children under 5, with one infant, only 5 weeks old at the time. He spent the next few months of his precious life alienated and crying in his home. He was no longer emotionally able to continue with his life normally or even do activities with his children. His hopes for recovery and healing were destroyed with many observing that in many ways, this person had already 'died.' Such is the power of doctor-patient relations. Healing through words is just as important as healing through the scalpel. The Australian medical profession must consider this vital aspect of emotional, spiritual and psychological healing and look at healing from a holistic perspective. The holistic perspective does not just exist in the Middle-East, but also has a strong historical presence in Asia with European and Western patients embracing its success and associated belief systems, even though their own Medical professionals have yet to incorporate its ideas in any constructive manner.

Educating society about making more effective medical

decisions should predominantly be a government responsibility and not just the responsibility of traditional educational institutions. Government campaigns that create awareness on the importance of being more proactive in making effective medical decisions can also help reduce government spending on healthcare in the long run. Free information available on interactive websites can potentially reach millions of Australians at once and provide them with crucial information that may one day save their life or the life of a loved one. Being proactive rather than reactive towards the costs of increasing national health expenditure is the key to ensuring that all Australians receive adequate healthcare treatment in the long run and maintain a sustainable quality of life. Information available on websites of medical professionals cannot be relied upon solely as they offer insufficient information and tend to only focus on the professionals' areas of interest rather than their success rate with particular surgeries or other vital information which may give clues about their effectiveness as healthcare providers.

While the use of a Medicare referral service which refers patients to surgeons with short waiting lists for surgeries in public hospitals aims to reduce public waiting list times, it does little to actually educate patients about making appropriate medical choices or ensure that the right surgeon is matched to the right patient. This potentially jeopardizes patient outcomes for complex cases which need specialist surgeon interventions. More attention needs to be given to matching patients with the correct surgeon and details regarding the pros and cons of public/private treatment options should also ideally be explained through the referral line if needed to allow patients to make more informed choices.

Thus, a more proactive education system which leads to

improved health literacy and critical skills that enable individuals to achieve improved health outcomes will not just relieve our increasingly overburdened healthcare system, but improve the quality of life and productivity of all Australians, whether or not they have fallen into the Medicare Nightmare.

Chapter Six: Who is responsible for the Medicare Nightmare?

From being a patient to being the health minister, we are all consumers and stakeholders in our national healthcare system and have a role to play in addressing the confounding Medicare Nightmare. Patients, government bodies, healthcare professionals including surgeons, physicians, nurses and health insurance companies can all contribute to help alleviate this national tragedy simply by confronting the key problems associated with poor information flow and limited access by health consumers to timely information that empowers them to make safer decisions.

Health insurance companies can play a significant role to help facilitate more effective information flow between patients and healthcare professionals, especially as they can significantly influence which healthcare provider one can access and influence patient choices with their 'no gap' arrangements. Linking 'no gap' arrangements with surgeons success rates may not just by itself improve patient decision making but also insurance providers profit margins as well. Insurance companies can wield- and do wield such power to influence their member's decision making through varying financial rebates for selected health professionals.

As health insurance premiums have been steadily rising over recent years, health insurance has become consequently less affordable, with some postponing their membership and others just scraping through to pay for their premiums. Rising insurance premiums though have not just been due to increasing costs by healthcare providers and inflation, but due to the fact that as a society, our overall well-being has been deteriorating. While there is a limited role that health insurance companies can play to prevent individuals from being diagnosed with terminal conditions such as cancer, there is much that they can do to help their members' access relevant information in order to find the most suitable and skilled surgeon or medical professional for their needs. Health insurance companies should question why some of their members are having the same surgery performed repeatedly, as this is a clear warning sign and obviously not in their interests nor in their members' interests.

Despite the fact there is a limit in what health insurance companies can do to help low income Australians afford their health insurance products (other than offering various limited cover options), there is a key target market that health insurance companies have not effectively tapped into. This target market would not just help relieve our healthcare system somewhat if they adopted private health cover but would *readily* do so if they properly understood the '*what's in it for me?*' factor. I will refer to this target market as the 'fence sitters.' These fence sitters will ponder often about the benefits of having health insurance cover and are somewhat interested in being covered. However, there are many factors which may delay their decision to adopt private cover such as:

- Having good health in the present which increases their complacency to take action

- No immediate need for health insurance products including extras

- Unsure of differences between health insurance products due to perceived complexity in product information

- Poor basis of understanding health insurance products, with opinions mainly formed through ambiguous communication with friends or some gossip chain

- Unsure of actual out-of-pocket expenses

- Find it difficult financially to pay for health cover but are willing to sacrifice other things in their life to be able to afford it, should they feel they need it

- Timing of decision clashes with other crucial decisions they must make which are also financially costly and competing equally for their attention and limited time

- Disadvantaged by unstable employment so feel unsure whether or not they can afford to pay their health insurance premiums in the future

- Have several unstable factors in their life which constrain their actions such as accommodation, family arrangements etc.

- Suffer from considerable stress in the present so unable or unwilling to risk committing to something new

- Their partner is either indecisive or reluctant to commit to having health insurance cover

The '*what's in it for me?*' factor is often poorly addressed by insurance companies who tend to promote the tangible gains of having health insurance over non-tangible benefits such as having greater peace of mind or more control over one's health outcomes. There is significantly more that health insurance providers can do to improve their marketing communication by more explicitly clarifying what their health insurance products have to offer potential members who have not been taught in their school education nor life experiences how to effectively differentiate between complex health insurance products.

Furthermore, by becoming advocates of patient and health consumer rights, health insurance companies will not just win the trust and business of more customers, but they will also reduce their losses and costs due to their members selecting ineffective treatment options, services and medical professionals. It is thus in the interests of health insurance providers to become more proactive patient advocates to improve their image in the public's eyes, convince 'fence-sitters' to commit and improve their financial returns in the long run.

Until now, there are few if any official avenues health consumers can turn to when they need to make critical medical decisions promptly. This provides health insurance companies with an opportunity to provide patients with vital information and take some responsibility for the dissemination of medical information. This does not mean that they need to accept liability for offering such services, but that they simply help facilitate information access for their members and health consumers in general. Whether they offer such useful information through referral services, counselling services or simply by including a few relevant hyperlinks on their corporate website for members, efficiency in the healthcare system is certainly a concern for all stakeholders. Simply by utilising existing advertising avenues such as websites, online magazines and newsletters, health insurance companies can help advise their patients how to minimise surgery risks and maximise treatment outcomes. This may not sound as glamorous as advertising articles on the benefits of super foods and diet fads but the patient bubble of ignorance and misinformation must be burst eventually. It is only through directly addressing patient treatment risks, that health insurance providers can genuinely protect their members from a potential health crisis and avoid excessive claims which drive up insurance premiums for all and reduce health insurance affordability.

Considering that health insurance companies may own some private hospitals, direct information should be more easily accessed by them regarding surgeons' success rates and customer satisfaction responses within their hospitals. Without an effective feedback loop, health insurance providers cannot improve the efficiency of the services that they support. Information collection from members may include patient questionnaires or answering a question such as how the hospital services they have recently used can be improved in just a few hundred words. Incentives may also be offered to members to enter a competition to win an attractive prize. Such questionnaires when run effectively can cost health insurance companies only thousands to run but save them in return tenfold what they spent gathering simple feedback. This is because there are some surgeons in the private hospital system whose surgical skills are questionable which results in several more, albeit unnecessary hospital admissions for members of health insurance providers. As these surgeons are not just harming patients but are also significantly impacting on health insurance providers' bottom line, this issue needs to be proactively addressed from both a business and ethical perspective. Prevention initiatives which monitor surgeons' results are crucial for both health insurance companies and government organisations alike as unsuccessful surgeries lead to further costly, unnecessary hospital admissions for patients and adversely affect all stakeholders in the health system. Such an initiative may predictably clash with healthcare providers interests as healthcare providers may object to easier access to damaging information on their treatment success rates; on the other hand indiscriminately supporting healthcare providers' rights over patient rights can potentially threaten the sustainability of our entire national health system. Ultimately, if we are genuinely interested in helping to save Australians from the traumatising Medicare Nightmare and our health system from eventual failure, then this is a key issue that must be addressed, making the cooperation of healthcare providers in releasing their treatment statistics more justifiable and crucial.

To date, patients have been punished in Australia for the inefficiency of our hospital systems through constantly increasing health insurance premiums and Medicare levies. Lacking both power and information to make unregretful medical decisions, it is time for other key stakeholders to support health consumers in avoiding more infinitely unique versions of the Medicare Nightmare.

Some patients do manage to overcome this power inequality through sharing useful knowledge in online forums; however such forums while potentially providing valuable information can also be accessed too late, give ambiguous advice or simply lead to panicked reactions in anxious, unskilled users.

Health insurance companies can facilitate information flow to health consumers by offering information research facilities and helping match members to suitable and reliable support groups. It is clear that unless health insurance companies become more proactive as key information providers, they risk making health insurance affordable to only niche consumer markets in the future. Furthermore, should the average healthy Australian cease to be able to afford health insurance, excessive future premiums may become harder and harder to justify for the remaining users. Indeed, considering the speed with which premiums are rising, reducing unnecessary costs due to preventable claims in order to make private health insurance continuously affordable to the average Australian should always be a priority for all stakeholders in the healthcare system.

When patients are harmed through poor choices, the private health insurance industry also suffers, making networking with other stakeholders to gather and disseminate information to members necessary for the long-term viability of health insurance providers. Lobbying our national government to ensure that our healthcare system is more efficient through improved access to crucial information therefore becomes a national benefit for all.

Other mutually beneficial strategies and initiatives' health insurance companies can implement include being proactive as information providers to secondary schools by becoming potential sponsors of health education programs, especially considering the fact that secondary students will become consumers of their services in the very near future.

Educating students not just on the benefits of having a healthy lifestyle but also teaching them through workshops, the relevant life skills needed to become their own health advocate would not only create healthier and more independent health consumers of the future, but further promote health insurance providers as key healthcare figures in students minds. This also offers opportunities for future marketing and public relations for health insurance companies. Presenting workshops or presentations to secondary students that teach them skills to make effective and speedy decisions during health dilemmas can help empower and prepare students to be ready for the 'unknown' in their future. This 'unknown' could be a health crisis that begins simply from injuring ones knee while playing soccer-it does not need to be generated from something genetic, age-related or even predictable.

Ultimately, health insurance providers must recognise that many Australians *are* interested in health insurance and that the intangible benefits available could be more effectively marketed. Health insurance providers can offer more than just financial rebates for different ancillary services- they can help save Australians from an emerging national tragedy that at least to some extent can be mitigated. As key stakeholders in the healthcare system, they must also ensure that they simplify their complex products where varying health cover and out-of-pocket expenses are concerned. Simplifying terms and conditions for insurance products and services while providing members and healthcare consumers with useful medical information, potential referrals and support group contacts makes it easier for 'fence sitters' to make timely decisions and improves the image of health insurance providers in the public eye.

Health insurance companies are also in an ideal position to promote 'holistic healthcare' solutions which Australians are increasingly turning to. The increasing number of naturopathy and acupuncture clinics across Sydney for example, reflects an increasing interest and demand for such services. Health insurance companies can leverage the fact that they offer rebates on such services unlike the public health system to not just increase their membership numbers but promote holistic wellbeing as well. Some Australians have become disheartened with the failures of western medicine, especially the failures of surgical intervention and instead prefer to seek treatment through more holistic avenues. Health insurance companies can be key information providers where the benefits and latest research on holistic treatments are concerned. They can advertise and share such information not just through their own sources but through health and wellbeing magazines and other avenues to reach natural health enthusiasts, who have increasingly become a strong target market.

Government can also play a significant role to help make our healthcare system more sustainable through ensuring that resources within the healthcare system are allocated more efficiently. Government must look at spending in the healthcare system with the view that 'it is better to be safe than sorry' rather than 'cut costs indiscriminately to save money.' The real cost of inadequate medical treatments in our nation is significantly underestimated as victims traumatised by the Medicare Nightmare are rarely captured by the statistics. The real questions we need to ask and therefore statistics we need to focus on are 'how many patients are currently seeking medical treatment as a result of failed previous medical treatments which have exacerbated any pre-existing health conditions, yet could have been avoided had they been initially dealt with effectively under the right surgeons hands?' The significant cost of hospital readmissions must be weighed up against up-skilling registrars and having more consultants available in theatre rooms for complex surgeries especially in university affiliated teaching hospitals. One must ask, is the government really saving money by having a patient re-enter emergency rooms on a yearly basis, having more than ten additional surgeries to undo the damage of the first surgery or becoming dependent on welfare payments as they find themselves constantly out of work due to the ongoing effects of the first failed surgery and paying less tax as a result of being able to work less? Looking at the health system in simplistic terms is short-sighted, especially if we continually reduce critical public discourse on our health system to whether or not we should spend more/less on a system that is essentially responsible for our national wellbeing. Naturally as the Australian population increases, we *will need to* spend more on our health system, the same way we will need to spend more on public infrastructure. The real debate therefore should not be simply centred on the question 'should we be spending more or less?' but how can we more efficiently spend money on our healthcare system? How can we address the black hole in our healthcare spending budget? Not considering the domino effects of an inefficient healthcare system on other government systems such as tax and welfare not only harms individuals trapped by the Medicare Nightmare but national productivity as well. Government bodies should also work together with other stakeholders such as patients and health insurance companies to improve information access by healthcare consumers who are disempowered by tight legislation which makes it difficult to sue, despite the fact consumers lack access to basic, vital information that aids effective decision making on their health in the first place. The Liberal approach of punishing public patients through less quality care, reduced rebates or slashed public healthcare spending is not just questionable ethically but ignores the real causes of the wastage in our Medicare spending. Providing poor quality care in public and private hospitals in the present is a huge future expense for our entire healthcare system and other government systems which must also manage its 'spill-over effects.'

Healthcare professionals can contribute to addressing the Medicare Nightmare by realising that it is also in their best interests for patients to be treated by the most appropriate medical professional for their needs. Even if one cynically alleges that it is in the interests of healthcare providers that members of the public remain unwell and dependant on seeking medical treatment, it is certainly not in their interests to be sued or lose professional credibility in their medical field. This is particularly so in the area of IVF, where big business may be blurred with delivering just, appropriate services to others. Unfortunately, one may be faced with resistance when calling on medical professionals to contribute and improve the information flow in their field by providing their actual success rates with various surgeries, especially if their success rates are not very impressive. Some surgeons will argue that exact figures are difficult to estimate due to other factors at play that impact on surgery success such as a patient's age and other pre-existing medical conditions; however having some kind of statistics available with explanations for variations is arguably better than having none at all. Some medical professionals even feel offended and reluctant to disclose sensitive information when directly questioned about their skills, when it is only human that no one is perfect at everything in any field.

One of the controversial reasons medical professionals in the private sector can fail to provide patients with adequate medical treatment is unfortunately greed. For example, in Alison's case, one obstetrician was more interested in charging her for unnecessary ultrasounds (which were not covered by insurance) than reading her referral letter. Another obstetrician failed to send her to a more apt surgeon for 'joint care' until it was clear that she was going to needlessly lose her baby- again. Acting in the sole interests of ones' patients as a core professional value unfortunately is not always practiced in the medical field. Reflecting on one's performance includes a realistic assessment of ones strengths and weaknesses in any field and healthcare professionals must always question which surgeries they perform well and which they should forward on to more apt surgeons. This involves contacting patients whose surgery was not successful, following up what went wrong and acting upon the information. Regretfully, none of the healthcare professionals Alison had encountered contacted her for feedback or modified their practices despite the fact she later met several women who had also suffered tremendously under their negligent care. Healthcare professionals must take more responsibility for the power imbalance between themselves and their patients and ensure that they are not just familiar with their peers' success rate with similar surgeries but that they justly refer their patients onwards in a *timely* manner. Such a task may regretfully be difficult for some to do due to having an overconfident nature, which has them continually attributing their failures to external factors and depending on private patients for their main source of income. However, as vital stakeholders in the Medicare Nightmare, their accountability must urgently be given more attention.

The power of individuals to help increase the efficiency of our Medicare System by helping its users make more informed choices cannot be underestimated. Managing and sharing information using online forums and groups has been the main avenue for many volunteers and patients who like to either provide advice or seek aid from others to make more informed personal choices. Individuals have therefore been a hidden, valuable resource for improving the efficiency of our health system through their voluntary contributions when networking through social technologies. There is also a growing and emerging trend that can be identified with the increasing adoption of social technologies; many patients and their advocates are forming informal collaborative networks to help them make more informed health decisions, meaning that there is a strong need to both share health information in our modern technology oriented society *and* access valuable information from similar patients to help make more effective decisions. Notwithstanding that this creates room for information dissemination, it also creates the risk of *misinformation* if social technology users do not have the necessary skills to analyse whether specific health advice is sound or even suitable for their needs.

Individuals are also powerful contributors as information collection by government bodies and health insurance providers relies significantly on their voluntary contributions and feedback. Understandably, some Medicare Nightmare victims may be too traumatised to continuously share their horrific experiences, creating psychological barriers for information collection and sharing. The government may perhaps help minimise this by offering incentives for individuals to manage specific social networking sites to help other Australians suffering from similar health conditions recover. Some Australians have realised the value of being members of international health support networks and have voluntarily established their own local Australian group- at their personal expense. Acknowledging work by individuals such as Kylie Bolan, who used her own traumatising experiences with Asherman's Syndrome to create a local Australian Asherman's Syndrome support group online can encourage others to similarly volunteer and improve the sustainability and usefulness of such online support groups. Such health activists have helped numerous Australians prevent health tragedies with almost no support and recognition from government and business whatsoever. The value of such forums can be demonstrated with women suffering from Asherman's being able to discuss their success stories with using complex combinations of western and eastern treatments; for example, acupuncture combined with *specific* vitamins, hormonal treatment and certain surgeries by *specific* surgeons to maximise treatment outcomes. Holistic and integrated treatment plans such as this are difficult to receive from one healthcare professional alone. This is because even if a surgeon has effective surgical skills, they may not be familiar with the benefits and successes of such integrated approaches, unlike patients who have physically experienced successful treatments using socially endorsed, holistic and effective strategies. The potential for individuals suffering from multiple complex health conditions to benefit from information on integrated health solutions is significant. There is still much that western medicine does not know about using integrated eastern and western health remedies and by the time it catches up to recognise such benefits, many people would unfortunately already have missed out on experiencing *holistic* health. However, current research has already proven at least in *some* areas of health, that eastern remedies combined with western remedies yield better results for patients than western remedies alone. For example, it has been found that women who undergo IVF treatment and have acupuncture treatment close to the day of embryo transfer have more successful results with implantation. According to one Acupuncture IVF support clinic in Australia, there is substantial research that supports the idea that women who struggle to become pregnant and utilise acupuncture treatment, experience significantly improved chances of becoming pregnant. Although many women enthusiastically testify that this is true, many IVF specialists are also reluctant to make such an assertion. The discrepancy between what is happening in the Australian medical field and patients lived experiences combined with the extensive variation in opinions of healthcare professionals in terms of what constitutes effective medical treatment, emphasizes the need for more proactive healthcare consumers who take ownership of their personal health and become their own health advocates.

This creates an immediate need for individuals to have new, sophisticated, tech-savvy skills to facilitate and enable their information collection and dissemination activities. Individuals tend to act as information providers for others and information collectors for themselves. Unfortunately, as statistics on medical professionals' success rates are often too difficult to access, individuals face considerable barriers to information collection even though they may enthusiastically engage in information dissemination using social technologies. Such challenges faced by patients when selecting the most appropriate surgeon for their needs at critical times, forces them to resort to dangerous, mechanical trial and error approaches and costs the health system considerably in the process.

Other initiatives individuals can take to gain ownership of their health and improve their own health outcomes and help others include:

- When selecting a health insurance product, patients must be aware that health insurance companies can affect which healthcare providers patients can afford through their rebate system, making choosing a more comprehensive health insurance provider essential for those with complex health conditions

- Knowing ones rights, for example, in a life threatening situation, being prepared to request an experienced trauma centre over a small local hospital

- Keeping a notecard with physician names, contact details and family contacts always on hand, especially if one is elderly or has a condition that makes them prone to losing consciousness and thus unable to make crucial decisions when necessary

- Ensuring that one's physician is board certified in their field of expertise

- Searching online for lawsuits filed against a particular physician one intends to use (while being aware that most patients do not sue for previously stated reasons)

- Asking healthcare professionals the right questions and trusting ones instincts to change their healthcare professional if their rational concerns are dismissed

- Understanding the structure of the public health system should one wish to be treated by it, which includes knowing the difference between attending physicians, consultants and registrars and when to ask to see one over the other

- Acknowledging that while one can collect information from various sources, the ultimate choice is theirs to make and they are responsible for what happens thereafter

Faster access to quality, timely health information and statistics is the key to avoiding both an individual and national Medicare Nightmare as physically trialling various health professionals is both time consuming and incredibly costly for both individuals and the healthcare system. I question the ethics behind the significant barriers and losses patients face when trying to access basic medical information and statistics that will enable them to make more informed choices in a technologically oriented society. Unless patients have timely access to such crucial information, they can face significant personal losses, prolonging and exacerbating their personal version of the Medicare Nightmare.

Chapter Seven: The future of our healthcare system

As Australia's economic relationship with Asia continues to develop, we can expect to see more holistic combinations of eastern and western medicine adopted widely and unofficially. This means that we will most likely be changing the way we look at healthcare solutions and medicine and becoming more open to embracing alternative eastern treatments which aim to heal the mind, body and spirit simultaneously. We can also expect variations between expectations on what holistic healthcare actually entails as Indigenous Australians view holistic health care as referring to whole communities rather than just bodies (Kelaher et al 1999).

Regrettably, dangerous political sensationalism has steered significant public discourse on our health system in a futile direction; emphasizing the need for more constructive public dialogue that will actually improve our national health. A more constructive and sophisticated perspective on how our healthcare system impacts on other government systems is central to any discussion on our national wellbeing and productivity. Through creating community awareness on the Medicare Nightmare, we accept our responsibility as individual stakeholders in the health system and realise that we *can* make a difference - by efficiently sharing vital information. This book creates greater awareness about the need for more coordinated information sharing- but ultimately it is up to the wider community to consider the issues raised as without collective commitment, any change and progress is limited.

Should no change occur, the sustainability of our healthcare system also becomes a key concern. The Business Council of Australia (2011) has recommended urgent action to maximise the health of all Australians to ensure a more prosperous nation and stated that productivity in the healthcare sector is relatively lower than other industries with costs rising faster than CPI, thus threatening the long term sustainability of our healthcare system.

Some of the market failures and weaknesses in the healthcare sector that the Business Council of Australia (BCA) has recommended action on and that have been identified by the National Health and Hospitals Reform Commission (NHHRC) include uneven distribution of health outcomes, clinicians preferring private practice due to few incentives for redistribution such as greater workplace stress in the public sector and greater policy attention to output quantity or demand rather than quality. Other reasons for market failure include lack of data availability on health outcomes and resistance to publishing such data, continued reliance on self-regulation by governmental and professional bodies and a lack of patient focus with few incentives for efficiency.

Furthermore, lack of treatment information, especially in electronic format on treatment options, costs and outcomes means that data collection on the degree to which our health needs are being adequately met is limited, inconsistent and untimely.

Weak investment in information technology including communication systems, significant errors and poor clinical processes have also hampered productivity and efficiency by up to 20 per cent in the healthcare sector. Australia's relatively higher hospitalisation rates and lower rate of CT and MRI investment by OECD standards will also demand attention in the long run. As the Productivity Commission's reviews suggested that there is a 25 per cent difference in costs between the best and worst performing hospitals, the BCA warned against blunt budget reductions and instead recommended that these challenges be addressed to make our health system more sustainable.

The immense logistical difficulty for health professionals to stay updated with industry knowledge and medical technologies and the gap this creates between best and actual practices increases the complexity for patients when making significant decisions and attempting to take greater ownership of their personal health. The BCA stated that consumer engagement in Australian health policy is poorly understood, inconsistently practised and requires ongoing organisational commitment if the future input of health consumers is to improve (Business Council of Australia 2011). However, consumers also need background information to contribute at the policy level, making increasing community awareness and knowledge of their intricate health system even more crucial.

In a win-win future scenario, increased consumer demand for good value and accountability can potentially lead to more rational and sustainable healthcare delivery, especially due to the rising expense of healthcare shifting more financial responsibility onto consumers. This will require fundamental changes in consumer attitudes and behaviours- that is a transformation from being passive to active health consumers with a high level of health literacy

(IBM Global Business Services 2006).

It is detrimental to our youth to not have them confront the reality that they may be forced to make serious health decisions by as early as their late teens, early twenties or thirties. They must confront the cold truth that the wrong decision about choosing who and where to be treated can cost them their future health, wealth and even families. Part of the Medicare Nightmare indeed is the silent overlooked suffering of individuals and the impact an unquestioned inefficient healthcare system can have on societies overall wellbeing and prosperity. The other side of the tragedy of the Medicare Nightmare is the failure to prepare our youth with the relevant knowledge and skills to face the most crucial decisions they will ever have to make in their lives. Assuming that our youth will somehow know what to do and who to turn to when a health crisis strikes ignores the harsh fact that health dilemmas often occur when we are least prepared to deal with them and least equipped with resources such as time and money. Diseases and illnesses do not discriminate with age, gender, beliefs or ethnicity. Certainly, young people are less likely to suffer from age-related illnesses such as heart problems and diabetes, but they do face a high risk of having sports-related injuries- which if poorly managed and treated in their early years can significantly impact on their employment options, mobility and quality of life in the future. If we continue to dismiss our responsibility to educate and prepare our youth to make effective future medical decisions in their life, then we are essentially automatically disempowering our youth to take *genuine* ownership of their lives. This is due to the reality that within 5-10 years of finishing secondary school, young people are forced to start making significant choices about health concerns such as back and knee problems or manage ongoing health conditions. Within 5-10 years of finishing secondary school, female students must make crucial decisions regarding their fertility, contraception and childbirth- which if poorly made will destroy any feminist dream they ever held. Students will need to be able to weigh up potential risks (which are not always clear) with any treatment plan they follow. Therefore, understanding the complex health system they will face and the range of health options they may encounter becomes essential knowledge for students and an obligation to teach for those responsible for educating them to be informed, active and healthy citizens within society. Skills such as paying close attention to often over-looked, small font on surgery consent forms which inform patients on how their surgery success may be jeopardized and understanding complex medical jargon used within a system they must effectively deal with- suddenly become *essential* survival tools.

The lack of follow-up of patients in the long-run means that misleading hospital surgery information or pamphlets are unlikely to be accurately updated as some side-effects do not manifest themselves till several years after the surgery date. This illustrates how medical information provided by hospitals can be easily misleading, incorrect and outdated and how we must empower ourselves as health consumers through networking with others to make more informed decisions. As surgery risks increase when performed by those with limited surgical experience, health consumers need to be confident that they have selected the most appropriate surgeon for their needs. An apt consultant that performs a particular surgery at breakfast, lunch and dinner time may offer better results than a professor who spends the majority of his time on research and has limited surgical experience. Other choices students will need to consider in their future include: should they opt for surgery, naturopathy or just wait and see if the pain disappears? Can they afford to wait, if so, how long? Even flu and fever symptoms when overlooked may become problematic in the future as they could be masking more serious health conditions with their ambiguous nature. Therefore, learning to use integrated analytical, interpersonal and literacy skills is necessary for enabling students to make the best possible decisions possible in diverse future health scenarios.

To mitigate the national Medicare Nightmare, health consumers must also lobby their government for increased treatment choices as health consumers and for ensuring that Australian surgeons are confidently skilled with the latest breakthrough surgeries and techniques in the medical field. Contrary to popular belief, Australia is behind in adopting many innovative surgeries and complex treatments meaning limited choices for its health consumers. Australia's healthcare sector is currently also still in the initial stages of appreciating and integrating healthcare solutions, especially those that combine eastern and western knowledge.

For example, progesterone injections are difficult to access in Australia despite being offered in most continents across the globe and only a limited number of Australian surgeons can effectively perform the complex trans-abdominal cerclage (TAC), and out of the few that are competent with this surgery-most are near retirement age. This also exacerbates the limited choices that Australian women may face and the consequence of having reduced power over their own bodies and lives. Similarly, ensuring that Australian surgeons are confidently equipped with the latest surgical skills in other areas of healthcare such as cardiovascular surgery, oncology and spinal surgery will potentially free many Australians from the clutches of the Medicare Nightmare and liberate them to live normal lives.

Ineffective surgeons who make significant medical errors often do so repeatedly- so unless one luckily stumbles across a past patient, the horror stories are hidden and one must inevitably learn the 'hard way'. The impact the patient-medical professional power imbalance has on individual's lives cannot be underestimated and overlooked. The significant power of medical professionals in influencing the treatment outcomes of individuals and the limited avenues patients have to sue when their health service providers make blatantly neglectful decisions *must* be balanced with improved access to crucial information which empowers patients to make safer and more effective choices. Information access immediately also becomes an ethical concern, considering that compensation for patients is hard to attain when they make misinformed choices and argue that had they had access to such pivotal information, they would *not* have suffered from such significant losses. Victims of the Medicare Nightmare face significant legal hurdles which impose time constraints on being able to access compensation and unless their surgeon has made a blatantly obvious error such as leaving a pair of scissors in their stomach, the legal obstacles make it difficult to establish a case of medical negligence within the limited given time frame which is usually only three years from the date of discovery that an error occurred.

Medical professionals must humbly accept that as no professional or individual can be perfect, they need to be more transparent about their surgical successes and failures. For example, as a biology teacher, if I branch out into other areas of science teaching such as physics *'out of interest'* and I find that half of my new students are failing and suffering from tremendous consequences, instead of trying to apply my skills more broadly, I should limit myself to biology teaching and recommend if possible, my physics students to another professional to teach them physics. Such simple decision making does not always occur in the medical field with some professionals' incredibly content to treat patients in areas they are not very effective in, providing that their misguided patients willingly consent.

The Australian healthcare system needs to act in its own best interests and not just in the interests of powerful lobby groups or medical professionals in the medical industry who significantly impact on its efficiency and yet enjoy extensive legal protection if they contribute to its failures. Innocent individuals should not be trapped and tortured by their Medicare Nightmare, but working and contributing in society like everyone else. There are many ways that we can facilitate information flow in our society to alleviate the national Medicare Nightmare and save individuals from being inflicted with debilitating trauma. In a technologically driven society such as Australia, significant costly barriers to basic information access should never exist. As healthcare consumers increasingly become more tech-savvy, they should also reap the benefits of having crucial health information at their fingertips when required. More proactivity and awareness in our society is needed to make such constructive information sharing a reality. Dismissing the need for such information sharing only prolongs the national and individual tragedy of the Medicare Nightmare and compromises the long-term sustainability of our health system. There is room for schools, universities, government bodies, businesses such as health insurance companies and natural health clinics to help contribute to improving the health systems efficiency especially as preventable deaths in Australia are occurring at a rate equivalent to a Bali bombing every 3 days (Richardson and McKie 2007).

As health professionals significantly underreport adverse events, healthcare consumers should be encouraged to report injurious medical experiences themselves to help prevent future errors on others, especially as more than 50% of all adverse events *can* be prevented (Shirley and Cockburn 2010). Patients must be educated to ask health professionals relevant questions; however patients are not often in a position to monitor the safety and quality of their treatment as they usually lack the necessary information to make informed treatment choices. They may feel powerless due to their health condition or simply feel confused in a new hospital environment (Braithwaite et al 2005).

It is well known that e-health systems have the potential to improve the quality of healthcare in Australia by facilitating the transfer of crucial and timely information such as a patient's medical history, allergies and current medications between healthcare providers, to enable more effective decision-making about individuals' health management and treatment options. Although the content of shared electronic records (sEHR) in Australia is somewhat unclear, information on diagnosis, treatment, referral and outcomes over time would be a vital national resource offering valuable information on the effectiveness of different treatment options and patterns between patient groups. This will potentially allow for more effective decision making in scenarios such as managing common conditions such as influenza and asthma which lead to thousands of preventable hospital admissions every year. Although some patients may fear privacy issues, such a move is necessary for both individual and national improvement in wellbeing. GP's have apparently shown support for such information collection and providing data if it can be proven that capturing information across different levels and sectors of the health system will lead to an improvement in the provision of health services (AIHW 2008).

Genuine public debate that will inform the decision making process of individuals rather than sensationalized media coverage is the key to improving national and personal investment in health choices. A lack of consumer involvement on the other hand results in continued rising costs and poorer levels of safety and quality in our health system. A commitment to easier health information access, greater accountability and transparency on the quality and safety of health services is needed to improve the overall performance of our health system. Commitment can be a key challenge as variations in quality care can also be attributed to competing health entities having few incentives to share best practice, a lack of clear health outcomes or performance indicators for health services and a lack of accountability regarding the quality of services offered to the public. Inefficient resource allocation and varying standards of care create significant costs for our health system, patients and taxpayers. Similar to businesses who value customer input and feedback on their products and services, the health system must have more ongoing communication with its consumers, rather than just being a passive service provider. Examples of community engagement include polling on significant issues, hosting citizen juries and co-developing through consultations appropriate performance indicators for the health system (Government of South Australia 2003). Health consumers can act as valuable partners that can improve national health outcomes where health promotion and the prevention of adverse events are concerned. Health consumers must acknowledge that as risks with health care increase, their health status may *not* always improve with further ongoing treatment and therefore they need to be more proactive and aware when managing their personal health. Limited resources for health care means that difficult choices must be made in the present by our society and the more we delay engaging health consumers in the debate on our health system, the more resistance such decisions may face in the future.

The increase in the use of hand-held technologies such as smart phones also means that social media networks will increasingly be used for gathering health information and finding social support by patients, such as those suffering from chronic and acute diseases and seeking valuable comfort from the sharing of symptoms and experiences. Social media networks have at least to a certain extent been able to provide valuable information to both patients and practitioners alike on care, diagnosis and treatment. Social networking sites have also been valuable places for clinical trial recruitment, professional training, public health campaigns and providing support for a salutogenic healthcare environment (Davis and Morrison 2012). Examples of support sites patients may use include Twitter (approx. 350 million users), Facebook (approx. 845 million) and Yahoo! Groups (approx. 115 million users).

As Australia moves towards a national electronic information health system, questions regarding information collection, access and benefits become even more crucial. Net benefits of the national e-health system are expected to be approximately $11.5 billion over the 2010 to 2025 period for both the Australian government and the private sector including households.

These benefits would derive mainly from the e-health system reducing avoidable hospital admissions and GP visits resulting from more effective medication management. The main idea behind the e-health system is that with more complete information on a patient such as Shared Health Summaries, Discharge Summaries and Event Summary documents, prescribing errors and adverse drug events which contribute significantly to avoidable hospital admissions can be reduced. Medical errors and costs can also potentially be reduced through maximizing the limited time patients and their healthcare providers spend sharing information. The national Personally Controlled eHealth Record (PCEHR) system however, has limitations due to expected reduced technology take-up by specialists and allied health providers compared to GPs, hospitals, pharmacies and aged care providers and the fact that it is based on an opt-in participation model meaning that the extent to which benefits are generated depend on the participation-rate by health consumers which in turn affects the participation rate of healthcare providers (Australian Government Department of Health and Aging 2013).

Although other e-health investments such as Electronic Medical Records, ePrescribing and eDiagnostics within Australia also have the capacity to increase the efficiency with which medical information is shared, we must take caution with the quality of information we collect and share and how this translates to not just faster and more accurate decisions by health professionals when prescribing medication but also more effective decisions by patients themselves when choosing between surgical and nonsurgical treatment options. A successful e-health system must also be able to inform health professionals to make better treatment decisions for their patients including administering timely referrals. Whether the e-health system will give health consumers *real* ownership of their health and empower them to make more educated decisions is still to be determined.

The eHealth system may make the health system more efficient where medication is concerned but offers little promise for health consumers who need assistance with finding the most appropriate health professional for their unique needs. It does not in any way provide a substitute for empowering health consumers through educating them to navigate their way through a complex healthcare system or finding the most apt surgeon for their needs. As the number of patients suffering from disabilities is steadily increasing in Australia, we need to be wary of how the inefficiency of our healthcare system is contributing to poorer public well-being and recognise that it is not a matter of hosting a public vs. private debate as poor health outcomes occur in both scenarios. For example, in Alison's case, the confusing career decision by a private surgeon she had contact with, to leave his private practise and join the public hospital system also contributed to poorer decision making on her part. As this particular professional was the only obstetrician that she could find that genuinely understood her unique case, having adequate care surprisingly required her to later yo-yo between being a private and public patient as this experienced health professional was unable to treat her as a private patient even though she had requested it! This complex choice was made after seeing several specialists in the private sector that did not understand her condition, misdiagnosed her and simply relied on guesswork rather than solid research and information, resulting in disastrous outcomes for Alison.

Such complex choices must sometimes be made and the stress of trying to make the right decision can often be incredibly draining. This raises important questions such as 'Do we have sufficiently trained professionals in the health system to treat difficult cases exacerbated by prior medical errors?' especially in situations where women face significant personal losses with the trial and error approach often used in medicine, especially in obstetrics.

There are many complex intertwining issues that need to be addressed when trying to improve the efficiency of our healthcare system. The goal of this book is to facilitate genuine public debate in order to confront the personal and national tragedy of the MN. One thing is clear however, patients cannot afford to remain passive health consumers but must be given the appropriate support and knowledge to make wiser choices that they will not later regret- not just for the sake of achieving better health outcomes, but more for gaining satisfaction in knowing that they made informed medical decisions rather than misguided ones. Addressing the Medicare Nightmare is *not* about perfecting everyone's health 100% (although in a Utopia it would be) but about empowering and supporting patients to make the best possible medical decisions for themselves and their dependents through taking greater ownership of the decision making process. This is because legally patients have already accepted such enormous responsibility, despite personally being unable to cope with the disastrous consequences of being uninformed passive health consumers. Unless we actively engage in a public debate on the difficult challenges we face in our health system, in the future we will be forced to make even more difficult decisions due to increasingly restricted health budgets which have been depleted by the increasing national health costs of poor individual decision making. It is only through initiatives that promote and embrace greater health information sharing, that we can help prevent more Australians from unnecessarily suffering from disabilities and alleviate the social inequality that results.

Successful health outcomes for all, need not be some illusionary goal rallied by idealists and social activists but a realistic attainable goal that can be achieved through a greater public awareness of the personal and national tragedy of the Medicare Nightmare. This means addressing the need for more efficient resource allocation both within and between government systems and recognising that blind cost cutting measures within the health system only serve to increase national health expenditure in the long term. There are also many ethical issues that also need to be considered in any proactive public debate such as whether low-interest or interest free loans should be available for Australians wanting private treatment but unable to afford it and whether we can simply invest in more preventative measures such as having more skilled consultants available to assist registrars in public hospital theatres to minimise medical errors during emergency admissions.

We must also address the idea that 'information *is* power' to rectify the power imbalance between patients and their health practitioners and empower health consumers to take genuine ownership of their personal health through having greater access to timely medical information.

It is only through proactivity and participating in national collective decision making and public discourse that we can truly make a difference in our health systems success. That is, it is only through the power of individuals and their active engagement with the systems that allegedly serve them, that any genuine improvement in health outcomes is possible. One thing is certain though, with Australian societies increasing reliance on technology including the current 'bring your own devices' approach promoted by the education system, crucial health information or data is potentially within the reach of our fingertips meaning that we really have few – if any excuses to find ourselves caught up in the pervading tragedy of the Medicare Nightmare.

Chapter Eight: Finding support through the Medicare Nightmare

If you find yourself or a loved one suffering from any of the five stages of the Medicare Nightmare, there are many issues that you will need to carefully consider regardless of the timing of the health condition. In general, the more complex your health challenge, the more sophisticated your research skills need to be to navigate through the vast array of information available through networking either online or physically. Ultimately, regardless of who provides you with medical information or advice, they will always caution you that they will not accept any responsibility should their advice somehow harm you or be misinterpreted by you. The fact no one else (including any support group, medical professional, government body) is willing to assume any responsibility over medical decisions made by you emphasizes the necessity for you to become your own health advocate. Whether you genuinely consent or not to carrying the burden of responsibility for the medical decisions you make is irrelevant as the Australian legal system forces you to consent to carrying such responsibility, regardless of your readiness to make significant risky health decisions. It is always assumed that when you do consent to any medical treatment, medication or surgery that you are fully informed of any risks involved, despite any other alternative reality.

There are also precautions that you need to take when analysing information that you find online. For example, while online health forums may be a great source of information, keep in mind that it is rare that any two patients' health conditions are ever exactly alike. Some information you come across may be beneficial for you, while other information you come across will simply make you feel more stressed and anxious. This is why knowing what *kind* of information to look for and *where* to look for it becomes essential such as referring to national groups- or transnational groups where the first is not available for more information. Referring to the latter group will also mean that you have even more information to filter through to find the right help or advice in your locality. Furthermore, knowing *where* to look will help overcome the burden and risk of information overload- where one is overwhelmed with too much information that results in excessive activity with minimum results.

As a patient, you have little choice but to play an active role in managing and taking ownership of your health. You will certainly feel the frailty of being a human being, especially if a medical specialist states that you have no chance of recovery. In such circumstances, you may need to look for a second health professional's opinion to ensure that the statement is not merely a reflection of the limitations of the professionals' skills and knowledge which can often be the case. This may mean inevitably 'specialist shopping' which has unfortunately become a necessity for many Australians to help locate the most appropriate health professional for their needs due to the difficulties faced when accessing basic information and facts from faster and cheaper avenues such as government bodies and online information sources. A significant warning however, is that when confronted with any stage of the Medicare Nightmare, you must give your condition the necessary time it requires to resolve itself and be adequately treated. You must be patient with this process as it could take weeks, months or even years to be completely resolved. In some unfortunate stages of the Medicare Nightmare, it may even never be resolved at all.

While struggling to cope with the Medicare Nightmare, you need to carefully revise your treatment options, determine your potential support groups (if any) and have a plan for finding potentially helpful health professionals. As the latter can often be more difficult, you may need to cautiously consider referrals from friends and GP's, as specialists in one type of surgery may not be effective in others, when surgical success rates come into question. In fact, if we consider the *actual* success rates of surgeons with various surgeries within their field, Australia's health professional shortage suddenly dramatically becomes a greater concern when effective outcomes are considered. You will need to question why the person giving the referral thinks that the referred professional is better than others. If a referral has been given simply due to it being the only person the referrer knows, it may become problematic and you may need to use the referral with caution. The human body simply cannot be treated like a motor vehicle. The mechanics approach to the human body of 'keep trying different things till we fix it' is costly and dangerous and can send you faster to the wreckers than any car model.

The first referral Alison received from her GP traumatised her before her condition was even confirmed. In fact, *most* referrals Alison received exacerbated her condition before she accidently stumbled upon the most appropriate surgeon herself. Furthermore, she found some of the health professionals' websites incredibly misleading in terms of the extent of the surgeons expertise and demeanour.

Ironically, one of the surgeons she encountered who did not even invest the time to read her referral letter and understand her condition, had a webpage emphasizing how much he takes great 'care' of his patients and how his 'uniquely' genuine 'care' is more exceptional than others in his field! Regardless of the fact he promoted himself as a philanthropist towards females, Alison found him very dismissive and careless with how he dealt with her case. Such excessive advertising claims must be dealt with using caution, especially as blurbs on professionals areas of 'expertise' or 'interests' rarely include raw data on the professionals actual success rates- especially if their success rates are dismal. Being misled by false advertising claims by such health professionals can easily make one feel like a laboratory guinea pig and subject one to disastrous consequences.

Thus, there are many issues for you to carefully consider when confronted with any stage of the Medicare Nightmare, such as:

- *Where* will you seek information from?

- *How* will you minimize the trial and error approach when trying to find the most suitable health specialist for your needs?

- *Who* will you turn to for support when struggling to cope within your family, friends and relevant support groups?

- *What* will you do in the event that you have gathered excessive information and yet no clear solution can be seen?

- *How* will you become your own health advocate and take ownership of your own health?

- In the event that your condition is poorly understood in the medical field, *how* will you empower yourself through your own research?

- *How* will you access information on surgeons' success rates with the specific surgeries you require, in the event you are advised that you must pay significant consultation fees to see surgeons and access such simple information? (*Please note: experience and number of surgeries is not the same as success rates with surgeries!*)

- *How* will you maintain your mental strength or a positive psychological outlook if the Medicare Nightmare jeopardizes your quality of life?

- *How* will you ensure that your stage of the Medicare Nightmare is not exacerbated through poor decision making on your behalf?

- *How* much time will you need to sacrifice from work and other life commitments to be able to adequately create an effective management plan for your condition?

- *How* might you benefit from interacting with support groups that deal with depression or your physical health condition?

- In the event, that the Medicare Nightmare threatens your career, family and future quality of life, *how* will you develop resilience and not lose your self-worth and confidence?

- *What* other areas of your life such as hobbies and passions will you engage in to balance the depleting and depressing effects of the Medicare Nightmare?

- *What* will you do if your contingency or treatment plans fail?

- *Do* you have the confidence to seek help effectively online, especially with navigating through discussion forums and analysing any information you find logically and carefully?

- *Does* your health condition allow you to take 'time off' from prolonged medical treatments that have depleted you of your mental energy?

- *Do* you have a need for holistic healthcare?

Mental coping strategies should also not be underestimated, especially as the mental suffering the Medicare Nightmare inflicts on an individual can often be more painful than the physical suffering itself. Self-blame is futile, especially when one realises that they were misinformed about their health professionals' competencies and in retrospect had limited choices to begin with. In such circumstances, it is important to note that the real tragedy of the Medicare Nightmare is not necessarily whether one's health has improved or deteriorated but the fact that one could have made better medical decisions had they been more informed in the first place. Even if one believes in the power of fate on our health in life, the reality is that we are still key players where health decisions and outcomes are concerned.

Formulating a 'recovery plan' as soon as you find yourself overwhelmed by the Medicare Nightmare is an essential survival strategy. In the very least, it will allow you to reflect more objectively on what has happened to you and help you to find the mechanisms with which to cope. A new recovery plan may need to be brainstormed after every adverse event as being yo-yoed between medical professionals can have a very debilitating effect on an individual's quality of life, making protecting ones mental health even more crucial. Guarding ones mental energy from a Medicare Nightmare is the most critical survival strategy as one cannot possibly make any effective medical decisions if they feel mentally drained and depressed. Furthermore, many stages of the Medicare Nightmare can literally destroy an individual's life creating significant stress associated with the insecurity of losing one's family, career as well as physical, emotional and mental well-being. A Medicare Nightmare recovery plan is not just about facilitating positive thinking but about structuring *clearer* thinking in order to develop more effective coping mechanisms and ultimately better overall health outcomes for an individual.

The goal of the recovery plan is to protect and preserve ones mental energy so that the destabilizing effects of the Medicare Nightmare do not further inflict one with psychological conditions such as post-traumatic stress disorders which make it even more difficult to cope with the everyday stresses of life. The need for a support group becomes essential for sufferers who feel alone, as it may be difficult for those around them to comprehend what they are experiencing, meaning that their pain and suffering is often underestimated and overlooked by those closest to them.

For example, a simple scenario such as failing to find appropriate medical advice and skills to correct a knee injury can affect ones career, meaning that they may be unable to work full-time, creating significant financial and emotional stress for one's family. This financial stress may be enough to destabilise their family unit and threaten their ability to maintain a family home. Not only must the sufferer face the future stresses of a limited and restricted work life but also potentially the significant risk of divorce and single parenthood, compounded by their inability to reduce stress and relax through engaging in sports and recreational activities they once enjoyed. This makes discovering and gathering one's inner strength more crucial, especially as many observers cannot imagine what victims of the Medicare Nightmare are experiencing unless they are unfortunate enough to experience similar losses themselves.

Medicare Nightmare Recovery Plan:

Goal for the next ….months   Date: …………

Places to gather information/
support………………………………………

Future treatment steps/priorities:

1.

2.

3.

Meanwhile, I will do activities I enjoy such as

………………………………………………………………………………

I still have hope because …………………………………………………

The stress the Medicare Nightmare inflicts on your personal relationships with significant others should also not be underestimated and must be given due attention. At times you may find that you desperately need relationship counselling, especially given that the Medicare Nightmare can destabilise even the strongest relationships. Considering the fact that most relationships are not as solid as 'Romeo and Juliet' in the first place and the existing high divorce rate in our society, the Medicare Nightmare can tip the relationship scales in the opposite direction as many partners or spouses find themselves no longer able to cope and remain supportive due to the long-term suffering it inflicts on them individually. Unfortunately, relationships often break down at times when sufferers of the Medicare Nightmare need emotional support the most, creating feelings of guilt, depression or anger.

There are many ways the Medicare Nightmare can impair or destroy relationships with significant others. Examples include:

- Friends feeling alienated why you don't call and communicate with them like you used to, creating divisive communication gaps between you and them

- Spouses being unable to cope with the draining long-term effects of the Medicare Nightmare on the family unit in the long run

- Dependency which forces you to be dependant one way or another on friends and family for a long period of time, making them feel strained

- Pessimistic and depressing effects on your character resulting in your company becoming less tolerable and enjoyable

- Being unable to maintain normal social or intimate romantic relations with the effect of pushing away loved ones

- Being forced to hide personal health details and events from those closest to you to avoid exacerbating feelings of discomfort and sadness

- Depression or mourning which has you preferring isolation over socialisation

Such effects of the Medicare Nightmare can be ongoing as even between treatments, the cyclical threat of instability and the perpetuating disastrous effects that the Medicare Nightmare inflicts on one's life, can easily encourage one to retract into a lonely cocoon to the bewilderment of their beloved family and friends. The alienating dilemma of the Medicare Nightmare where one feels not just misunderstood by health professionals but by their own inner circle of family and friends can be devastating to an individual's emotional health. Thus, maintaining relations with others even through remote communication becomes a necessity to help alleviate feelings of despair and loneliness. Your closest family members may also need to be counselled so that they do not accidentally reinforce any feelings of loss. For example, a cancer sufferer may feel depressed when there is too much discussion about the future whereas a woman suffering from recurrent miscarriage may feel alienated when she is surrounded by conversations that continuously focus on baby colic and other baby talk. If you find yourself suffering from the severe stages of the Medicare Nightmare and have been given few reasons to remain hopeful on the outlook of your future, being vigilant about the company you keep becomes more essential- even if it means consciously seeking out new friendships that allow you to momentarily forget the pervasive effects of your medical experiences on your life. As it is more difficult and certainly not ideal to avoid family members, it *is* ideal to be honest with them about your sensitivity to excessive discussion of certain topics.

In the event that your Medicare Nightmare is ongoing with no end in sight, you will also need to weigh up whether or not you can afford (financially and health-wise) to take a 'mental holiday;' that is time off treatment to allow your mind an opportunity to recoup itself, focus on areas of your life you actually enjoy and goals in your life that you have yet to accomplish. This will at least give you the chance to gather some strength and energy for the next 'round' of the Medicare Nightmare. Anything you can do to further build your confidence, whether it is to develop your skills or professional career will also help to empower you to face the unpredictable future that may lay ahead.

If you find yourself unfortunate enough to continuously experience random disastrous events in the process of seeking medical treatment, you need to be even more protective over your mental health. Reassessing what you *really* want out of life at this stage is essential as you do not want to waste your entire precious life languishing in deep self-pity or remorse. That would indeed be the ultimate tragedy. When facing the frailty of the human body, ascertaining the greatness of the human spirit in being able to triumph over adversity is a necessity. Building such resilience in your character may be accomplished through a variety of ways such as:

- Discussing with others who have been through similar significant adversity in their life, any effective coping strategies that they have used

- Reading about amazing people who have triumphed over various disabilities

- Reading self-help books about holistic health, positivity or alternative thinking

- Seeking psychological counselling

- Joining a faith based support group

- Confiding in a close friend or family member whose advice you value

- Dedicating time to activities and projects you greatly enjoy to remind you that there are things in life worthy of living for

- Connecting with a reliable support group for your health condition whether online or physically

The latter deserves special mention as providing that one's communication skills are adept- especially with navigating through online social technologies and websites, the key to escaping from a prevailing or future Medicare Nightmare may potentially or literally be at ones fingertips.

There are numerous support groups available that aim to support sufferers of similar conditions by allowing them to connect with others that have endured similar experiences. While naming and analysing the effectiveness and reliability of all available support groups is beyond the scope of this book, an overview of the diverse attributes of some existing support groups is given below. Note that these are examples only and are not to be relied on for medical advice due to the dynamic nature of support groups. One is always recommended to seek the advice of a health professional but perhaps in the event that one is unsure of *which* health professional to consider approaching, valuable information from the experiences of others with various health professionals can potentially be accessed through such support groups. Other groups and contacts listed below assist patients in avoiding the Medicare Nightmare by guiding them through choosing more adequate health cover, utilising medicines more cautiously and selecting support groups more wisely.

Chronic Pain Australia

This organisation consists of a group of volunteers including sufferers and health professionals who offer user-friendly, research-based information and support a forum that allows chronic pain sufferers to understand and control their physical pain more effectively through connecting with others living with similar debilitating conditions.

Cancer Connections

Cancer Connections is an online community that connects people with cancer, their carers and families with other survivors. It offers avenues for participants to both receive and provide support to each other to assist them to manage the challenges of particular conditions, allowing them to connect to sufferers in particular age groups or suffering from particular types of cancers. Considering the increasing prevalence of cancer in modern society, making correct treatment choices in a timely manner is very crucial for cancer sufferers especially as some terminal cancers such as stomach and pancreatic cancer are routinely diagnosed too late by medical practitioners due to their ambiguous symptoms which are often fatally overlooked.

ABC Health and Wellbeing

While not a support group, this website offers valuable information on finding suitable support groups (i.e. a consumer guide on patient support groups). It gives information on what to look for, questions to ask, pitfalls of consumer health groups etc. allowing one to make a more informed decision regarding whether or not a particular support group may actually benefit them.

Consumers Health Forum of Australia (CHF)

CHF is a peak organisation that aims to represent the interests of Australian healthcare consumers. They help promote the safety, quality and timeliness of healthcare for all Australians through utilizing available health information and communication systems in Australia. They represent approximately 427 health consumer groups and aspire to offer useful information for people living with chronic conditions. They also provide media information on the health system to increase consumer awareness on issues that may affect the quality of medical care that health consumers receive.

Choosing Wisely Initiative

Launched in April 2012 by the ABIM Foundation, with input from approximately sixty medical specialty societies in the US, this initiative allows consumers to compare certain decisions of their health professional with best practices from a list of 'choosing wisely' recommendations. This may assist both consumers and their health providers to make more effective and fairer choices through referring to information on when certain diagnostic or medical procedures are necessary. A similar information site in

Australia would help create a balance in the decision making process, potentially protecting consumers from falling into the Medicare Nightmare while avoiding placing unnecessary financial stress on the Australian health system. Until such local initiatives emerge, this American project may offer some useful insight.

Private Health Insurance Ombudsman

This is an online Australian government resource for helping individuals interested in private health insurance cover choose the most appropriate health insurance plan for their needs. The website of the Australian Private Health Insurance Ombudsman also offers an online questionnaire to help consumers narrow insurance options down and allow them to more thoroughly consider what type of cover they may require. This is an educational tool for both students and consumers as long as one remembers that when properly judging any health insurance plan, the 'devil is in the details,' such as which particular surgeons/professionals are covered and which are not.

Medicines.org.au

Considering the strong link between incorrect medication administration and adverse events, it is necessary for consumers to understand why they have been given specific medicines, especially when their medical professional has not explained the medicines purpose and contraindications thoroughly. This website offers the latest versions of product information and consumer information that is provided by pharmaceutical companies. It allows one to check complications and concerns they may have with taking particular medications prescribed and potentially avoid adverse events. In addition to advice obtained from pharmacists and medical professionals, this website may be useful to patients.

Ultimately, **information creates knowledge and knowledge creates power** which is essential to help counterbalance the lack of power Australian health consumers' constantly face in their healthcare system when attempting to make more effective health decisions. Considering the widespread, privileged technological access that our society enjoys over others, we have few excuses – if any to be trapped in the Medicare Nightmare and must empower ourselves and others through existing medical information that is untapped, overlooked and difficult to access. It is only through the more sophisticated individual and collective use of medical information and statistics that the Australian health consumer can truly be empowered and the debilitating national and personal Medicare Nightmare mitigated.

Efficient information flow between all stakeholders in our healthcare system needs to be at the forefront of any constructive national health debate so that more productive discourse can drive the direction of funding in our health system and ensure social justice for all. It is time for Australian health consumers to receive timelier, crucial health information that matches the burden of responsibility that they have often disastrously carried for decades when making significant health decisions. Furthermore, it is only when we are able to comprehend the concept of the Medicare Nightmare that we can then address the details in effectively managing our publicly funded health care scheme such as which health care services Medicare can afford to fund or withdraw funding from altogether. In addition to the problematized lack of efficiency in the

Australian healthcare system due to poor information flow, further areas outside the scope of this book which also impact on the availability of quality healthcare for all includes monitoring Medicare and private health fund fraud and mismanaged government spending in other policy areas such as counterproductive foreign wars and misdirected economic policies that exacerbate inequality in Australian society. All of these issues work together to constantly convince Australians that they need to settle for increasingly less in both their education and health, while compromising our most precious national asset in the process- our wellbeing. It is only through challenging and addressing how these factors work together to disempower the average health consumer that any genuine, constructive public discourse on our health system can be initiated.

Chapter Nine: Visual reflections on the Medicare Nightmare

Medicare Nightmare #1

Finally, we can say Doug has escaped his Medicare nightmare.
MN
MN
MN
Medicare Nightmare Ave
RiP Doug
MN #6278
THE END!
21 Choose your own MN adventure
Medicare Nightmare # 2

Medicare Nightmare # 3

Medicare Nightmare # 4

145

Medicare Nightmare # 5

Medicare Nightmare # 6

Copyright Dalal Oubani

The <u>Real</u> question

Medicare Nightmare # 7

Medicare Nightmare

Medicare Nightmare. # 8

Copyright Dalal Oubani

Well, you can relax Mr Singh b'cos I have experience dissecting frogs!
EMERGENCY WARD
Medicare Nightmare #9

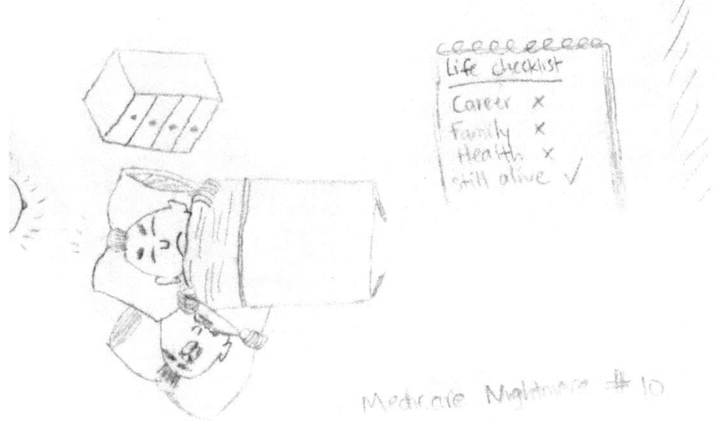

Copyright Dalal Oubani

The future of
savvy health consumers?

My smart phone is so smart it can even tell you how to avoid the medicare nightmare!

Medicare Nightmare # 11

Medicare Nightmare

Chapter Ten: References

- ABS (2010), *Consumer Price Index,* Australia, Catalogue No. 6401.0.

- ABC Health and Wellbeing http://www.abc.net.au/ health/consumerguides/stories/2004/08/05/1837060. htm

- Acupuncture IVF www.acupunctureivf.com.au

- Australian Institute of Health and Welfare (2008) *Review and evaluation of Australian information about primary healthcare: a focus on general practice.* Cat no. HWI 103. AIHW: Canberra

- Australian Institute of Health and Welfare (AIHW) (2013), *Australian hospital statistics 2011–12.* Health services series 50. Cat. no. HSE 134. AIHW: Canberra

- Ashermans Australia www.groups.yahoo.com/ group/AshermansAustralia

- Australian Government Department of Health and Aging (2013) *Expected benefits of the national PCEHR system,* The Commonwealth of Australia: Australia

- BOS (2004) Physical activity and sports studies

content endorsed course years 7-10 syllabus, Board of Studies NSW: Australia

- BOS (2012), NSW syllabus for the Australian curriculum: Science, years 7-10, Vol 2, Board of Studies NSW: Sydney p. 32-34

- Braithwaite, J., Healy, J., Dwan, K.(2005) *The Governance of Health Safety and Quality,* Commonwealth of Australia: Australia

- Business Council of Australia (2011), Selected Facts and Statistics on Australia's Healthcare Sector, BCA: VIC

- Cancer Connections http://www.cancercouncil.com. au/49274/cancer-information/general-information-cancer-information/when-you-are-first-diagnosed/ emotions-and-cancer/cancer-connections-online-support/

- Chronic Pain Australia http://www. chronicpainaustralia.org.au/

- Choosing Wisely Initiative http://www. choosingwisely.org/

- Consumers Health Forum of Australia (CHF) https://www.chf.org.au/

- Davis, K. and Morrison, R. (2012) *Future imperfect,* World Health Design: April 2012, Norman Disney & Young: VIC

- Government of South Australia (2003) *Better Choices Better Health: Final Report of the South*

Australian Generational Health Review, April 2003, Government of South Australia: SA

- Hunnam, M. (2010) *Healthcare Facts & Statistics Australia,* May 192010, http://www. resolvehealthissues.com/tag/healthcare-statistics-australia

- IBM Global Business (2006) Healthcare 2015: win-win or lose-lose? A portrait and a path to successful transformation, IBM:USA

- Kelaher, M., Baigrie, B., Manderson L, Moore L., Shannon C. & Williams, G., (1999a), *Community Perceptions of Health, Illness and Care: Identifying Issues for Indigenous Communities,* Women & Health, 28:1, p. 41-61

- Kelaher, M., Baigrie, B., Manderson, L., Moore, L. , Shannon, C. & Williams, G. (1999b), *Community Perceptions of Health, Illness and Care: Identifying Issues for Indigenous Communities,* Women & Health, 28:1, p. 50

- Medical error Australia http://www. medicalerroraustralia.com/

- Medicines.org.au http://www.medicines.org.au/

- Private Health Insurance Ombudsman http://www. privatehealth.gov.au/

- Richardson, J. and McKie, J. (2007) Reducing the Incidence of Adverse Events in Australian Hospitals: An Expert Panel Evaluation of Some Proposals ,Centre for Health Economics, Monash University: VIC

- Roughead EE, Gilbert AL, Primrose JG, Sansom LN (1998) *Drug-related hospital admissions: a review of Australian studies published 1988-1996.* The Medical Journal of Australia. Vol 168, Issue 8, p. 405-408.

- Runciman WB, Moller J (2001) *Iatrogenic Injury in Australia.* Australian Patient Safety Foundation: Adelaide

- Shirley, M and Cockburn, T (2010) *Implementing the open disclosure of adverse events in Australia through a Mediation Model,* paper presented at the Europe Pacific Conference, Cortina d'Ampezzo, Italy, 7-14 January 2010, Queensland University of Technology: QLD

- WHO (2001) Legal status of traditional medicine and complementary/ alternative medicine: A Worldwide Review, World Health Organisation: Geneva

About the Author

Dal Ouba, (Dalal Oubani) is an Academic Literacy Teacher who has achieved academic scholarship in the area of curricular justice in education after she published an academic article in 2014 on this subject for the *International Journal of Education (IEJ), Comparative Perspectives.* Her multidisciplinary approach to educational matters is attributed to the fact she has an extensive educational background in Medical Science, Business, Education and the Arts (TESOL). She has also contributed towards the development and revision of the Australian Curriculum for both the English and History syllabuses stages 4-6. With almost a decades experience teaching in the secondary education sector, Dalal specialises in teaching scientific and academic literacy and has created many quality literacy programs for secondary schools in Sydney. Dalal has also presented at international conferences on education and is currently the Director of *Accelerate Australia,* an educational website aimed at both complementing and assessing the impact of the Australian Curriculum on Australian society. As a certified workplace assessor and trainer, this allows Dalal to share her unique expertise with her peers, while contributing to improving the quality of the education system in Australia. Dalal currently teaches academic literacy across university colleges in Sydney and is commended for her professionalism in her field and highly regarded by her peers for her skills, especially developing unique and engaging educational materials that support student learning.